Ephesians, Colossians, and Philemon

INTERPRETATION
A Bible Commentary for Teaching and Preaching

INTERPRETATION
A BIBLE COMMENTARY FOR TEACHING AND PREACHING

James Luther Mays, *Editor*
Patrick D. Miller, Jr., *Old Testament Editor*
Paul J. Achtemeier, *New Testament Editor*

RALPH P. MARTIN

Ephesians, Colossians, and Philemon

*A Bible Commentary
for Teaching and Preaching*

John Knox Press
ATLANTA

Library of Congress Cataloging-in-Publication Data

Martin, Ralph P.
  Ephesians, Colossians, and Philemon / Ralph P. Martin.
      p. cm. — (Interpretation, a Bible commentary for
teaching and preaching)
  Includes bibliographical references.
  ISBN 0-8042-3139-7

  1. Bible. N.T. Ephesians—Commentaries.   2. Bible. N.T.
Colossians—Commentaries.   3. Bible. N.T.
Philemon—Commentaries.
I. Title.   II. Series.
BS2695.3.M36 1992
227—dc20   91-37588

© copyright John Knox Press 1991
This book is printed on acid-free paper that meets the
American National Standards Institute Z39.48 standard.♾
10 9 8 7 6 5 4 3 2
Printed in the United States of America
John Knox Press
Louisville, Kentucky 40202-1396

SERIES PREFACE

This series of commentaries offers an interpretation of the books of the Bible. It is designed to meet the need of students, teachers, ministers, and priests for a contemporary expository commentary. These volumes will not replace the historical critical commentary or homiletical aids to preaching. The purpose of this series is rather to provide a third kind of resource, a commentary which presents the integrated result of historical and theological work with the biblical text.

An interpretation in the full sense of the term involves a text, an interpreter, and someone for whom the interpretation is made. Here, the text is what stands written in the Bible in its full identity as literature from the time of "the prophets and apostles," the literature which is read to inform, inspire, and guide the life of faith. The interpreters are scholars who seek to create an interpretation which is both faithful to the text and useful to the church. The series is written for those who teach, preach, and study the Bible in the community of faith.

The comment generally takes the form of expository essays. It is planned and written in the light of the needs and questions which arise in the use of the Bible as Holy Scripture. The insights and results of contemporary scholarly research are used for the sake of the exposition. The commentators write as exegetes and theologians. The task which they undertake is both to deal with what the texts say and to discern their meaning for faith and life. The exposition is the unified work of one interpreter.

The text on which the comment is based is the Revised Standard Version of the Bible and, since its appearance, the New Revised Standard Version. The general availability of these translations makes the printing of a text in the commentary unnecessary. The commentators have also had other current versions in view as they worked and refer to their readings where it is helpful. The text is divided into sections appropriate to the particular book; comment deals with passages as a whole, rather than proceeding word by word, or verse by verse.

Writers have planned their volumes in light of the requirements set by the exposition of the book assigned to them. Biblical books differ in character, content, and arrangement. They also differ in the way they have been and are used in the liturgy, thought, and devotion of the church. The distinctiveness and use of particular books have been taken into account in decisions about the approach, emphasis, and use of space in the commentaries. The goal has been to allow writers to develop the format which provides for the best presentation of their interpretation.

The result, writers and editors hope, is a commentary which both explains and applies, an interpretation which deals with both the meaning and the significance of biblical texts. Each commentary reflects, of course, the writer's own approach and perception of the church and world. It could and should not be otherwise. Every interpretation of any kind is individual in that sense; it is one reading of the text. But all who work at the interpretation of Scripture in the church need the help and stimulation of a colleague's reading and understanding of the text. If these volumes serve and encourage interpretation in that way, their preparation and publication will realize their purpose.

The Editors

PREFACE

The writing of these pages on the so-called Captivity Letters has occupied my attention over the past few years, and it has been a rewarding experience to listen to and interact with the text with a specific purpose in mind.

But acquaintance with these letters goes back much farther, and I have had the opportunity of teaching these texts to several adult Bible classes in Southern California as well as to a succession of seminary students in their exegesis courses. I mention these historical notices not to draw attention in any trivial way but simply to share with any pastors or Bible teachers who may find a use for this book. What I have learned in church school and classroom has, I am sure, immeasurably enriched my understanding of the Pauline text. Whether I have been able to transmit these life-enhancing lessons through the written page is another matter. Readers will be able to judge for themselves.

The Captivity Letters are a rich deposit of Christian truth, waiting to be excavated and put to use in the church's ministry. Of the wide variety of topics presented whether by Paul or in his name two may be singled out: the cosmic dimensions of christological teaching and the role of the church as God's locus and agent of reconciliation. Both these themes stand high on the current agenda of theological and practical inquiry and planning. To hear again Paul's voice, direct and oblique, on such central matters is an exercise no minister or Christian leader should overlook. The following pages were first designed to aid in this enterprise and are sent out with the same intention.

It has been my good fortune not only to be helped by several generations of inquiring and interesting students but, in one particular regard, to have had their considerable cooperation at both the academic and the practical level. Phaedon Cambouropoulos, minister in Athens, wrote a Th.M. essay on the Colossian Philosophy; George E. Cannon worked with me on his *The Use of Traditional Materials in Colossians,* published in 1983; Daniel G. Reid, now Reference Editor of Inter-Varsity Press, offered a doctoral dissertation on "The Christus Victor

Theme in Paul"; and Erwin Penner, a professor in a Canadian Mennonite seminary, was awarded a Ph.D. for work on "The Enthronement Motif in Ephesians."

A special word of thanks needs to go to John McVay, Assistant Professor of Religion at Pacific Union College, Angwin, California, who began with me at Fuller Theological Seminary and followed me to the University of Sheffield, England, in the interests of his work (in progress) on the role of the church in Ephesians. His labors in producing a readable typescript and checking references have been commendable, and I gladly pay tribute to his rare diligence and skill.

CONTENTS

EPHESIANS

CONTENTS

PHILEMON

BIBLIOGRAPHY

To
Colleagues in the Department of
Biblical Studies
The University of Sheffield

Hommage de l'auteur

THE BOOK OF
Ephesians

Introduction

An Epistle for Today

No part of the New Testament has a more contemporary relevance than the letter to the Ephesians. Its importance as God's message to the modern church has been recognized in a variety of ways.

The teaching on the universal role of Christ in creation and redemption is high on the agenda of ecumenical concerns. Ephesians sounds the note of celebration that the Lord of the church's worship rules the entire universe and that in him God has a plan to embrace all the nations and all orders of existence.

At the same time, this letter faces the reality of evil which still presses upon human life both personal and societal. The author's vision, to be sure, is bounded by the horizon of Christ's cosmic victory and all-embracing triumph. Yet he still is enough of a realist to know that the church and the world are plagued by evil powers which must be resisted and overcome.

The liturgical overtones that punctuate the letter suggest an indebtedness, on the author's part, to snatches of hymn, creed, prayer, and sacramental idioms that he has built into his pastoral writing, thus giving it a distinctive flavor. Recent study has focused on the rhetorical features that govern the shape and flow of his argument and appeal as he seeks to win over his readers. That may be so, but there is no denying the impressionistic appeal that dominates the letter. He expects his hearers (as the letter is meant to be read out in worship services) to be fired by the same doxological outbursts that he rehearses and to be thrilled, as he evidently was, with the news of God's amazing

1

grace in reconciliation and re-creation. The notes of celebration and doxology are much needed in modern worship, and Ephesians is the letter best suited to help our liturgy to reach this end.

A final appreciation of Ephesians reminds us that Paul's ministry continued after his demise, and in the hands of his faithful disciple it attained a new dimension, since Christian truth is never static but always applicable to new situations.

But why should the would-be preacher turn to Ephesians for pulpit messages, when some of these concerns seem remote because the epistle's thought world (of two levels of existence) and apparent triumphalism are hard to relate to without considerable adjustment? The answer has to be that such effort is worthwhile. To be faithful to the full range of the New Testament's witness to Christ and his church we must try to grapple with ideas that seem, at first sight, to have little pragmatic and practical value.

Only as we are prepared to see the letter on its immediate first-century background will we have a springboard and point of entry into our modern interest. As the following sections of the introduction will attempt to make clear, the author's governing thought of Christ-in-his-church has to be viewed as his response to the twin threats of a historical circumstance and a theological novelty appearing on the scene. The history relates to the disappearance of national Israel with its temple cult, following 70 C.E., and the problem posed by a church membership now predominantly non-Jewish. The theological innovation is seen in a Gnostic worldview that drove a wedge between God and the creation and looked to astrology to gain access to life's security.

On both counts the author finds his solution in the cosmic Christ who is *both* the answer to ethnic rivalry and tension by his work of reconciling Jews and Gentiles to God and to one another *and* the key to a mysterious and hostile universe.

Given these two presuppositions, it is not difficult to see some direct relevance to the Christian pulpit in our day. Racial tensions still lie unresolved in local neighborhoods as well as on a giant scale in South Africa. Human beings are still menaced by fear of the unknown and uncertain future, and they find solace, in the face of life's problems and the threat of death, in the occult and in superstition.

This letter offers an apparently simplistic response to press-

2

ing needs. In Christ, who is now Lord of the cosmos and the destined final point toward which history is moving, God has spelled out a concern for the world and its people. But the simplicity of the letter is its genius. As we base our proclamation on these supports we will find an entrée into the inexhaustible wealth of this tantalizing letter.

The Purpose, Occasion, and Background of the Letter

"The Epistle of Paul the Apostle to the Ephesians": so runs the sonorous caption in the superscription attached to this document in the Pauline corpus according to the KJV. Yet no part of this full description has escaped the critical probe. Each item in the heading—Is Ephesians a letter in the attested Pauline sense? Is Paul the author? Is this document addressed to the congregation at Ephesus?—has been questioned and defended almost to the point of stalemate. Markus Barth confesses to a set of enigmas that hang over Ephesians when he says that it "comes to us as a voice of a stranger" in a chapter aptly entitled "A Stranger at the Door: Paul's Puzzling Epistle" (p. 9).

Of the three parts of the traditional designation two may be mentioned only briefly, for a virtual consensus has been reached that (1) Ephesians is not an epistle in the usually accepted sense of the term, that is, an apostolic letter to a Christian congregation in a specific area; and (2) the destination of the epistle is much wider than the local Christian community at Ephesus in the senatorial province of Roman Asia. Moreover, the epistolary framework is artificially constructed to conceal a general treatise that has no specific class of readers in view. This remark has to be qualified, however, by noting the author's interest in the needs of the audience.

The absence of personal greetings is remarkable, and the suspicion that the author's relationship with the readers is strangely impersonal and indirect—so unlike that of the Paul who wrote to the Galatians and the Philippians—is all but confirmed to the hilt in 1:15 and 3:2.

This observation leads to the question of the text of 1:1. Our doubts that the "letter" was sent to Christians at Ephesus—or at least solely to them—based on the evidence that the writer knows his addressees only at secondhand, are reinforced by the textual uncertainty of the words "at Ephesus" (Gr. *en Ephesō).*   3
Most scholars conclude that no name stood in the original text. If the document was composed as a circular letter, intended to

be passed around to a group of churches, there is no reason why such geographical place(s) should have been left out. They are present in I Peter 1:1. Perhaps the original version of the encyclical had a blank space for the insertion of a place-name. There is some evidence for this practice in ancient court circular letters, adduced by Günter Zuntz (p. 228 n. 1). So Ephesians may well have been composed more as a homily than as a pastoral letter addressed to a local congregation. The textual exemplar that contains "at Ephesus" at 1:1 is that copy which survived in the archives of the church in the metropolitan capital of western Asia. We will return to this proposal.

Having granted that at least two of the three issues raised by this "epistle" have been virtually settled in scholarly debate, we are still left with the more thorny matter of authorship. The present writer has argued ("An Epistle in Search of a Life Setting," pp. 296–302; and *New Testament Foundations*, vol. 2, chap. 18) that it was a well-known disciple and companion of Paul who published this letter under the apostle's aegis either during the apostle's final imprisonment or (more probably) after his death. He did so by gathering a compendium of Paul's teaching on the theme "Christ-in-his-church," and he added to this body of teaching a number of liturgical elements (prayers, hymns, and confessions of faith) drawn from the worshiping life of the apostolic communities with which he was himself familiar. The purpose of the epistle was to show the nature of the church and the Christian life to those who came to Christ from a pagan heritage and environment and to remind the Gentile Christians that Paul's theology of salvation history never disowned the Jewish background out of which the (now predominantly) Gentile church came.

We may well imagine what prompted this manifesto when we study closely the chief emphases of the letter. Two such are the requirements that the call of the Christian life is to the highest levels of morality, both personal and social (4:17; 5:3, 5, 12), and that Gentile believers who enjoy rich privileges as members of the "one body of Christ" can never deny the Jewish heritage of the gospel without severing that gospel from its historical roots. Hence the epistle's insistence (2:11–12) that the messianic hope meets all the needs of its Gentile readers (3:6). Though they were converted to Christ later in time than their Jewish fellow believers (1:12–13), they are in no way inferior on that account. Rather, the privilege they now have binds them

4

indissolubly to their Jewish counterparts in the family of faith; both groups share in the Holy Spirit of messianic promise (1:13; 4:30).

The point seems to be that Gentile Christians, who were streaming into the church, were adopting an easygoing moral code based on a perverted misunderstanding of Paul's teaching (cf. Rom. 6:1–12). At this same time, they were boasting of their supposed independence of Israel and were becoming intolerant of their Jewish brethren and forgetful of the Jewish past of salvation history (cf. Rom. 11).

This epistle effectively checks these two wrongheaded notions and does so by displaying the true meaning of Christ's relationship to the church. He is its head and Lord, so requiring loyal obedience and service; he is the bridegroom, seeking a pure bride; and he is both Israel's Messiah and the Gentiles' hope, so uniting in himself a new people, both Jews and Gentiles. To be sure, these distinctive features of the letter are not altogether unique to Ephesians, and Paul's disciple has faithfully conveyed the substance of his master's teaching. Yet he has angled it in such a way that its thrust is set in the direction of the erroneous doctrine and practice that he seeks to dispel. Much of the letter will take on significance if we can endeavor to see it as a magnificent statement of the theme "Christ-in-his-church," yet presented and applied in such a fashion that false ideas and wrong ethical conclusions are rebutted.

At this point we return to the question, Is Ephesians addressed to the church at Ephesus? Clearly it is difficult to believe that Paul would write in an impersonal and roundabout way to a Christian fellowship he had lived and labored among for some considerable time (Acts 19:10; 20:17–38). On the face of it, this "letter" is no ordinary pastoral address sent to a specific congregation or group of churches.

This fact is confirmed by the textual uncertainty of 1:1. The words translated in KJV "at Ephesus" are lacking in the leading manuscripts (Sinaiticus and Vaticanus) and in the Greek papyrus known as P46, dated about A.D. 200. It is likely, then, that this document was composed as a circular letter to the churches in a wide region—Asia Minor being the most probable location, in view of the affinities with Colossians—and that either it was carried from one place to another in the area by a courier or (in view of the later textual authority for the place-name of Ephesus) the author left a blank space in the superscription, to be

5

filled in as the messenger handed over the particular copy to the church. There are some difficulties with this reconstruction, but on balance it seems to be the most plausible view.

If we rightly judge the epistle to be an encyclical addressed to the Gentile churches in Asia (3:1), this estimate helps to account for the style which is influenced by a liturgical, rhetorical, and catechetical strain. Directly personal allusions may not be expected in a document that is more accurately described as an exalted prose-poem on the theme "Christ-in-his-church" than as a pastoral letter sent to meet the needs of a particular local congregation. The author breaks out into an elevated meditation on the great themes that fill the mind—God's purpose in Christ, God's fullness in Christ, Christ's fullness in the church which is his body. Concepts like these lift the writer onto a plane of rapture and contemplation which is evidenced in the language used. Rare terms may well be drawn from the worship of the (Asian) churches. Certain elements of style (such as the prolific use of the relative pronoun, the construction with participles, and a fulsomeness of expression) are clearly those of a typical early Christian liturgy.

Central Ideas of the Letter

As a document addressed to a perilous situation, this letter is full of Christian instruction of great importance. The author is gripped by what is virtually a single theme that runs like a thread through his treatise. He marvels, as a true disciple and follower of the great apostle in whose name he writes, at the grace of God which has brought into being a united church. In this Christian society, Jews and Gentiles find their true place (2:11–22). The unity of this universal society which is nothing less than Christ's body (1:23; 3:6; 4:4; 5:30) is his great concern (4:3–5).

The author starts from the premise of "one new person" (2:15) in which a new humanity has been created by God through Christ's reconciling work on the cross (2:16). By this achievement in relating humankind as sinners to God, Christ has brought Jews and Gentiles into God's family (1:5; 2:19; 4:6; 5:1) as children of the one Father. The coming into existence of this one family where all barriers of race, culture, and social status are broken down is the wonder that fills his vision. The earlier Pauline teaching of Gal. 3:28–29 and I Cor. 12:12–13 is now filled out, extended, and its lessons drawn and applied.

There is a new slant put upon the apostolic teaching, how-

6

ever, which marks a novel phase of development in the doctrine of the church. One factor is the way in which Christ and his church are regarded as a single entity. The head-body metaphor, which is familiar to us from the earlier Pauline letters, takes on a new dimension in that the head becomes inseparable from the body. In I Corinthians 12, Paul had insisted on the indivisibility of the body, which is made up of many members (cf. Rom. 12:4–5), but in Ephesians (notably in 1:22–23; 4:15–16; 5:29–30) the head and the body are inextricably united and interdependent.

Another important statement about the church's nature comes in the attributing to it of a sort of transcendental status. The church shares the heavenly life of its exalted Lord even now in this age (1:22; 2:6; 5:27), and the distinctive features of the church in this epistle are akin to those classically stated in the creed: "I believe in one holy, catholic, and apostolic church." That is, there is a timeless, idealistic quality about the church's life which says more about what the people ought to be than what they actually are in this present world.

Yet the epistle knows that the church lives an empirical life in this world and that its readers face pressing dangers. They are counseled against allowing their pre-Christian moral standards to decide and control their present conduct (4:17–24). They are put on their guard against pagan teachers who would undermine the Christian ethic they accepted as part of their new life in Christ (5:3–6). Baptism is appealed to as a dramatic summons to rouse from moral stupor and a call to walk in the light of holy living (5:14).

The seductions of those who were leading the readers astray with empty words (5:6) and causing them to be tossed about by crafty dealings (4:14) suggest the presence of a type of "gnosticizing" teaching. Basic to the Gnostic worldview was a dualism that drove a wedge between God and creation and regarded the latter as alien to God (see the Introduction to Colossians later in this volume). It insinuated that men and women could safely ignore the claims of morality and (in a strange paradox with both elements attested in second-century Gnosticism) either indulge their bodily appetites without restraint or treat their bodily instincts with contempt. Thus both libertinism and asceticism are logical consequences of the principle that God is remote from matter and unconcerned about what men and women do with their physical life.

Because of such teachings the writer is moved to give warn-

7

ing against a cluster of evil practices (5:3, 5, 12) and to argue for resistance to the pull of degrading influences (2:3). He is equally concerned to defend the value and dignity of marriage against those who, from false ascetic motives (cf. I Cor. 7; I Tim. 4:3), would depreciate the marital state. But his real answer to these false notions and practices is to deny outright the dualistic basis of the teaching. This denial is carried through by an insistent statement of the church's heavenly origin and earthly existence. The incarnation of Christ and the elevation of redeemed humanity are two powerful facts to which he appeals for his conclusion that heaven and earth have been brought together into harmony (1:10).

By the same token of cosmic unity, the "gnosticizing" tenet that humankind is held in the grip of a relentless and pitiless fate is effectively challenged and overthrown. The answer to this element in Hellenistic religion is found in the eternal purpose of God, whose will embraces those very cosmic powers— the eons—which the first century most feared (3:11). It was the divine plan that Christ should cause these spiritual beings which Greek astral religion thought of as holding lives in thrall to lose that hold upon men and women (3:9–10). God did that by raising his Son from death's domain and placing under his feet the entire universe, including these cosmic agencies (1:19– 23). He has exalted the church, too, above these powers and so lifted Christians beyond the range of cosmic tyranny and bad religion (1:22; 2:1–10; 5:8, 14, 27).

Christ's victory at the hands of God, who raised him from death, is at the very heart of the theology and cosmology of the epistle. Yet the question presses, How do believers come to share in this conquest over evil powers? The New Testament answer is that in baptism they "put off" the old nature (4:22–24) and so die to the rule of these malevolent powers (Col. 2:20); at that time they "put on" the new humanity with corresponding Christlike qualities. This feature explains *both* the hinge—represented by the baptismal chant of 5:14—on which the author's practical and hortatory counsels turn (5:3, 8) *and* the admonitions he addresses to his readers to be renewed in the image of the new Adam (4:17–24).

The experience of baptism (in 5:26) marks the start of a new life of holiness to which this epistle summons its readers. The letter warns them to shun the specious doctrines of "gnosticizing" libertinism with its disparagement of the body and calls

8

them (in 6:10–18) to stand bravely against those evil powers which are ranged against them. They are potentially defeated foes of the church, but victory will come only as Christians are diligent in the use of the armor that God has provided and prove the reality of their conversion and baptism by standing firm in the Lord. The eschatology, which in other places looks to be totally fulfilled in Christ's ascension and enthronement, here makes room for an element of a "not yet completed" dimension.

In summary, the epistle teaches the cardinal doctrine of the God who is all-powerful and all-wise in the loving design God has for the world. Christians, who share the risen life of Christ, are raised above the pitiless control of cosmic forces which would treat humans as playthings of "fate" and "luck." Equally they are lifted onto a high plane of noble living that opposes all that is sensual and debasing. The conflict they engage in is a sign of the reality of their new life, begun in the conversion-baptism experience.

The church is the historical witness to God's renewing purpose. Originally centered upon Israel, a nation elect for the sake of humankind, that purpose now embraces the Gentile peoples. Both races find their focal point of harmony and understanding in the creation of a new society, "one new person" (2:15), neither Jew nor Greek but Christian (see Lincoln, pp. 605–624). Here is the clear articulation and extension of Paul's thought in I Cor. 10:32 and the foundation of the later Christian claim that the church forms a "third race" of human beings who, reconciled to God through Christ, are united in a new way to realize a new society of men and women and to be a microcosm of God's ultimate design for a broken and sinful race.

OUTLINE OF THE EPISTLE TO THE EPHESIANS

INTERPRETATION

Praise and Thanks in the Light of the Church's Salvation

EPHESIANS 1:1–23

The body of the letter opens on a magnificent note of jubilation and with an outburst of praise. The reasons for such a doxology are then rehearsed and center in God's sovereign plan to call God's people into being. This design, we learn, antedates creation and was brought to realization in history with the coming and sacrifice of God's Son. Christ's achievement is the centerpiece of the church's exaltation, which the text celebrates. Yet the writer's concern is personal and pastoral. The rehearsal of what God has done once in history merges into a tribute to the readers' share, made real by the ministry of the Holy Spirit who has applied the benefits of redemption to human lives.

The author's own involvement is seen in a prayer report, giving thanks for the readers' response. He calls on them in this indirect fashion to realize to the full the wealth of the spiritual treasures now made available by the enthronement of Christ as head of the universe.

Ephesians 1:1–2
Address and Greeting

The pattern of letter-writing practices in the ancient world is followed in this opening. The writer's name is given first. The Christian distinctive is seen in the note of authority sounded with the phrase "an apostle of Christ Jesus by the will of God." The use of Paul's name is intended to claim apostolic sanction for what follows and is in line with his practice of appealing to his vocation as one who had a special ministry in the churches.

11

The basis for that vocation is Paul's having seen the risen Lord (I Cor. 9:1) who charged him to fulfill a ministry to the Gentiles. The ground is thus laid for what will come in 3:1–8, namely, Paul's role as apostle to the non-Jews par excellence, which in turn gave a basis for the Pauline mission after his death.

The writer, in Paul's name, greets the readers, whom he does not know personally (see 1:15; 3:2), under the titles of their Christian standing. They are "the saints" and "the faithful"— two terms borrowed from the simpler text of Col. 1:2. The Ephesians author uses these two parallel terms to designate the role of Christians as God's holy people in tandem with Israel (Exod. 19:5–6; Lev. 19:1–2; Deut. 7:6; 14:2) and as faithful believers in the messianic salvation. "In Christ Jesus" denotes the sphere of their existence as incorporate in the new society, a theme elaborately worked out in 3:6.

For the reasons behind the omission of "at Ephesus" from the RSV and most modern translations, see Introduction, section "The Purpose, Occasion, and Background of the Letter." The two Greek words are lacking in the leading manuscripts and in the important papyrus known as P46, dated about 200 C.E. Moreover, early Christian writers endorse or imply the view that "at Ephesus" was not found in the earliest texts. The textual evidence is not easily explained, as Ernest Best, who provides one of the clearest expositions of what the data and the various amendments and translations have to offer, concedes (see his chapter "Ephesians 1:1," *Text and Interpretation*, pp. 29–41). The three main options are (1) to render "to the saints who are (also) faithful in Christ Jesus" as representing the original text, which a later copyist altered by the addition of "in Ephesus"; (2) an attempt to supply an emendation, made by Richard Batey (p. 101), who wants to propose an original reading of "to those who are *in Asia,*" which a later scribe garbled as "the saints" by mistake; and (3) the most plausible option (in our view), which sees the two expressions "saints" and "faithful" as parallel terms, perhaps representing the two wings of early Christianity: Jewish believers called the "saints" in Rom. 15:25–31 and Gentile Christians dubbed "the faithful" (so Caird). But no single translation is wholly satisfactory or does justice to the Greek once "in Ephesus" is left out to expose the original text. There is a consensus that the earliest manuscripts lacked this place-name; but the conundrum of how to render accurately the remaining Greek words once the variant is removed is not yet resolved.

The greetings of "grace" and "peace" are traditional to Pauline prayers (I Thess. 1:1; I Cor. 1:3; Gal. 1:3; Phil. 1:2). "Grace" is the saving action of God to redeem and restore the creation which has gone awry from God's purpose; the effect is seen in "peace," the attainment of harmony and wholeness (akin to *shalom*) as the new order reflects its unity with the Creator's plan, seen in 1:10.

Ephesians 1:3–14
The Purposes of God in Eternity and Time

The opening of the epistle is both like and unlike some Pauline and non-Pauline precedents. We may compare II Cor. 1:3–11 and I Peter 1:3–9. The common elements are the Praise to God formula, based on the synagogue liturgy and practice of ascribing "blessing" *(berakah)* to God for creation and redemption, and the fulsome descriptions of God's character as initiator of blessings bestowed on the people. But the dissimilarities are clear, too. In the earlier Second Corinthians and (probably contemporaneous) First Peter, praise to God glides into a recital of personal concerns and addresses the readers in their situations. Ephesians 1:3–14 stays on an exalted and somewhat detached plane, and little is said about the readers' own circumstances until the second part of the letter's body (notably in chaps. 4 and 5).

There are two or possibly three approaches to these stately verses. First, we may detect a chronological sequence. The plan of God is rehearsed in its "historical" shape, beginning with the Father's eternal purpose (1:4), proceeding into the way it was worked out in history by Christ's redemptive ministry (v. 7), and completed later in human experience as the readers are brought onto the scene (vv. 13–14) and are shown how they became believers in Israel's Messiah. The thought flows along temporal channels as the author views the entire range of God's salvific purposes from a past eternity (v. 4) to future realization (v. 14). According to this understanding, the concern is to express in heavily loaded theological idioms the manner in which the divine plan was originally conceived in God's eternal counsel and brought to actuality in Christ's achievement in human history. By this one act in time (v. 7), the forgiveness of sins was

13

secured for all believers (v. 13) who were brought to faith by their hearing the Pauline gospel and responding to it. The transition from historical redemption to its application in personal experience is made possible by the work of the Spirit who gives to believers now (v. 13) a foretaste of completed salvation in anticipation of the end time (v. 14). There are some parallels in Jewish worship with this style of reciting "the saga of salvation," and it may be that the model is taken over and christianized to adapt it to Gentile audiences.

Second, by picking up the same clue of a Jewish synagogue pattern, we may opt to see the passage, which is full of hymnic and poetic features (e.g., the Praise to God formula; lots of relative clauses and participles; in fact, these verses are one complete—if convoluted—sentence, strung out to massive length), as borrowed from a current Christian liturgical format. This, in turn, is modeled on a trinitarian layout, reflecting the praise of God in the threefold revelation and drawn from the worship practices of the Asian churches. To be sure, the trinitarian pattern is rudimentary and essentially functional, but it is suggestive to see here the triad formulations of God's activity. It is the Father who chooses his people in love (vv. 3–5). The one in whom the church is elected is Christ the Son, who is also the redeemer at the cost of his sacrificial death (v. 7). It is the Holy Spirit who applies the work of Christ to his people and so makes real in human experience the eternal purposes of the trinity (vv. 13–14). According to this view, the text is laying the foundation on which later creeds and liturgies will be formed; out of these raw materials will be fashioned the Christian belief in and confession of "one God in three persons." This may be so. Yet the present passage is still a long way from a set creedal statement, and it shares more in the exultant outbursts of praise that go back to the enthusiasm and charismatic freedom that characterized the Pauline congregations.

We are not driven to select one or the other of these approaches. The hymnic literary style of the passage is well evidenced, as indeed is the way the flow of thought moves from past to future. So it may be that the salvation history model is the key, while incorporating a specimen of early Christian liturgy. One other factor is just as germane. The set piece, whatever its pre-history or liturgical antecedents, may have been put in place at the opening of the document as a proem, that is, a short summary of what is elaborated later, and as an attempt to begin to address the readers' problems.

14

There is, then, as a third option in our approach to the opening section, a polemical purpose in the writer's assembling of these liturgical materials. The intention is to counter the rival claims that Jewish believers were in some way superior to their Gentile counterparts. The latter also are assured (in vv. 13–14) that they too are included in Christ, even though they were not the first to hope in Christ (v. 12). On a broader front the writer's purpose may be to call on the Christian belief in divine election (vv. 3, 11) to answer the charge that life is at the mercy of unseen yet powerful cosmic forces and that fate or chance ruled the world. On the contrary, he asserts, God's final goal in history is to sum up all things in Christ (v. 10), who is claimed as the rightful Lord of creation and the fulfillment of the human and cosmic story (see too 3:9–11 for a similar assertion of God's plan for the "ages"). A background such as this may ease some difficulties that surround the traditional teaching on election and predestination, clearly brought to the surface in verses 5 and 11 and that the interpreter will need to address.

Election is here set in a contextual framework. The author's thought begins with God whose purposes in eternity are the starting point of all Christian praise. The thought is governed by a desire to anchor the church in the divine plan, since its real life-in-God, called "the heavenly realms" (in v. 3, NEB), is the hidden agenda of the epistle's ecclesiology. We may look ahead to 6:12, where the same theme, in a different key, is picked up.

The church now lives "in Christ" (v. 3) because of God's premundane choice which effectively ensures the human response in faith to the proclamation (cf. II Thess. 2:13). This is indeed a mystery, and to some people a stumbling block. Yet it is undoubted New Testament teaching. Some preliminary comments will prepare us for a few guidelines through a dark terrain. The negative aspects of election (sometimes referred to as "the doom of the damned") which developed later are not much in evidence in the New Testament and are not found at all in this text. Unless we do have some assurance that God is behind and within all our pastoral endeavors, we shall be driven to an unhealthy and frustrating reliance on those endeavors as the best we can do to discharge our ministry. We see this frenzied activism in popular evangelical and church growth movements in our day. All the weight of responsibility is placed on "what we can do," and success or failure is dictated by circumstances we confront. Thus, two kinds of hearers are popularly regarded as "whosoever will"—and "whosoever won't." But

15

this is too facile, since it overlooks the divine factor, which poses the problem of election. Here, then, are some helps, drawn from the early church's teaching.

First, the New Testament writers proclaim God's electing mercy not as a conundrum to tease our minds but as a wonder to call forth our praise. The present passage is set in a liturgical context, which means that what is set down is intended to inspire the adoration of God. Second, they offer this teaching not as an element in God's character to be minimized or apologized for but as an assurance that our lives are in God's hands rather than in the grasp of capricious fate and iron "necessity" (as the Greeks in their pessimistic moments thought). First-century Hellenistic religion, under the bane of astral religion, knew this fear, expressed by Gilbert Murray as "failure of nerve" and put into poignant verse by some modern poets:

> I, a stranger and afraid
> In a world I never made.
> A. E. Housman

> Strong God, which made the topmost stars
> To circulate and keep their course;
> Remember me, whom all the bars
> Of sense and dreadful fate enforce.
> Hilaire Belloc

Third, the emphasis on election is never stated as an excuse for carelessness in spiritual matters but is coupled with the reminder that Christians have a moral responsibility to make their "calling and election sure" (II Peter 1:10, NIV) by accepting the highest moral standards. We are chosen to be "holy and blameless" in God's sight (v. 4).

Once we can orient the teaching in the light of its setting, and relate God's final outworking to bring the disparate elements of the cosmos into harmony with that purpose (v. 10), the rest of the section falls into place.

A threefold division is both logical and chronological.

1. The Father's choice (1:3–6)

Election is intimately connected to adoption (v. 5), and both designs are expressions of his love. His intention is that there should be many sons and daughters in his family, all of whom share the likeness of the elder brother (Rom. 8:29; cf. Heb. 2:10).

So naturally Christ is known as "the beloved," the one whom God loves. This is a messianic title in Judaism (cf. Mark 1:11), but the nearest parallel looks to be Gen. 22:1–8, which, some claim, Paul has in mind in Rom. 8:32.

2. Christ's achievement (1:7–10)

Becoming and being a Christian depends on what Christ has accomplished, called in verse 3 "every spiritual blessing." That phrase is now unpacked. Redemption looks back to Israel's bondage in Egypt and God's deliverance (Deut. 15:15) and to release from Babylonian exile in Second Isaiah (Isa. 43:3; 52:3). The new exodus is made possible by the cross where Christ's blood (i.e., his life given gladly in obedience to the Father's will, as Heb. 10:5–10 shows) was offered. The immediate benefit is forgiveness of sins, with the promise that, since the burden of the past is removed, a new start to life is begun. Spiritual vision is bestowed as believers come to see and respond to God "in all wisdom and insight."

Redemption and pardon are but a part of the entire work of Christ. What is termed "the mystery of his will" (v. 9) embraces the universe in its scope; it is a plan to be put into operation when the appointed times (Gr. *kairoi*) have run their course. The nature of that plan is now stated. It has as its grand objective the summing up of all things in Christ (v. 10). The verb (Gr. *anakephalaiōsasthai*) is difficult. The root meaning is "to sum up," to gather up under a single head as a tally at the end of a column of numbers or a conclusion in an argument *(kephalaion),* and so present as a whole (Rom. 13:9). Here it probably means that in Christ the entire universe will one day find its full explanation and rationale, its "principle of cohesion" (Caird). If so, this bold claim marks the completion of New Testament thought which has Christ as the source (Col. 1:16; John 1:3–4; Heb. 1:2–3) and the sustainer (Col. 1:17) of creation. He is now hailed as the destined Lord of all life as the goal toward which the whole creation is moving, until it reaches its omega point (to use Teilhard de Chardin's term).

We may well suspect the presence of some counterteaching in Asian churches (e.g., that which lies behind the Colossians letter) which prompted this response. False teachers, opposing the Pauline tradition, were claiming a secret instruction which was open only to a privileged few. This centered in their pos-

17

sessing the clue that unlocked the mysteries of the universe, a first-century kind of scientology. They congratulated themselves on their self-styled wisdom, insight, knowledge (*gnōsis*, in Greek; hence "gnostic"), and access to the "mystery" which revealed the hidden truth of the universe. They were intent on guarding this private information and keeping it within the circle of initiates.

Paul's followers castigate this pretension. By deliberately availing himself of the very terms and language of the rival teachers, the author opposes current notions. The secret of the divine purpose is in Christ, and it is an "open secret" accessible to all believers. It is and remains a mystery in the sense that no human intelligence could have guessed what God planned to do; but it is now revealed to Paul and his group (see 3:3–6). Its content is that Gentiles as well as Jews are united in a common hope and blessedness, with all racial barriers broken down (2:11–22) and all specious claims to exclusivity exposed. Paul grasped this universal note of the gospel in his ministry; now his disciples celebrate it in opposition to all who would restrict its scope to a coterie of the elect. Election is still a serviceable (and necessary) term, but it is universalized to include all who are in Christ, the cosmic savior and reconciler of the universe, not simply a "bouquet of believers" (P. T. Forsyth's phrase). Verse 10 fits in well with this response.

Gnostic errorists here, like their counterparts in the next century, drove a wedge between heaven and earth and taught that God had contempt for alien matter. The essence of Gnostic religion is dualism. The Pauline reply, assuming the Hebraic stance that Yahweh made the earth and man to reflect his image, is to state that the cosmic Lord who came from God to man is now exalted to the divine presence. In so doing, he has bound heaven and earth together into a unity. There is no aspect of human society or sentient life outside the scope of this reconciliation and no hostile forces, to be mentioned in 6:11–18, that can frustrate God's eternal purpose. In fact, the church's proclamation to these cosmic powers (in 3:10) states their inclusion in the divine scheme and so neutralizes their power to harm believers.

3. God at work in human lives (1:11–14)

From these somewhat detached and erudite matters, however needful to establish his point, the writer turns his mind to the process by which God's saving design touches human experience. He joins himself to the Jewish people who had long been sustained by the hope of Messiah's coming (v. 12). The discussion comes to a turning point at verse 12. By writing "you also" (v. 13) he broadens his appeal to include the Gentile readers he is addressing. The intention is deliberate. He is leading up to his statement in 3:6 that *now*—in the new age of Messiah's appearing—ethnic and religious connotations have lost their meaning. Both Jews and Gentiles are "members together of one body" (NIV) to form a worldwide church, even if they did come into that body from differing cultures. The Jewish people "obtained an inheritance" (v. 11, NRSV; NIV alters this verb of "inheriting") in the sense of assigned a role to play in history and taken to be God's special possession (Gr. *klēros*). The Gentiles had no such privilege and place, but in Christ both units of ancient society gain in unison their destiny of becoming God's "inheritance" (Gr. *klēronomia*). Jewish privilege is thus broadened to include all nations.

The way into the church, however, is the same for both groups. The process is outlined in verses 13–14, with several steps marked out. Hearing the word of truth, that is, the Pauline gospel (cf. Col. 1:5), is the first way forward. This message is defined as "the good news of your salvation." There is emphasis here on *your*, as good news to the *Gentiles* who are now embraced in the messianic salvation offered to the Jewish people. They responded in faith, as a second step indicates. The third term, "the sealing of the Spirit," is more problematic, since the idiom is a metaphor. In fact, there is a cluster of metaphors all gathered together in a couple of lines: you were sealed by the Holy Spirit of (messianic) promise, who is the "deposit" (NIV, rendering *arrabōn,* a term for a commercial down payment or first installment on a purchase) of our inheritance (*klēronomia,* looking back to v. 11 and so binding the beginning and the ending of the short paragraph) until we acquire (full) possession of it. We must supply *full* because the inheritance has already begun to be enjoyed by the Spirit's gift. What lies ahead is the final redemption, of which Paul wrote in Rom. 8:11, 18–25. This Romans passage may be set alongside the present section,

19

linked as it is by several common ideas and terms. The outlook is futuristic, yet that future may be faced with confidence, since hope is always in the New Testament "good hope through grace" (II Thess. 2:16) and fastened to the reality of God's power and providence to bring to completion what has begun.

The prospect, then, is one of a final redemption, already initiated in the offer of forgiveness and new life (v. 7) and awaited with eager yet restrained composure. The nexus of "now . . . not yet" runs as a major theme through the theological and pastoral thinking of all the New Testament writings—a rare observation of the unity that does exist amid prevailing diversities of expression and idiom. God's saving purposes in Christ have already appeared in the life of the church, but the end is not yet. For Ephesians the end is not even in sight; but the final chapter of God's story, while it may contain surprises, may be guessed from what has happened and is continuing. Christ is exalted; the church is alive and raised with him (1:20–23; 2:6); there is still conflict to be faced (6:10–18) because the days are evil (5:16). Yet the end is not in doubt, since the Spirit lives in the church as a guarantee that "final inheritance," a term drawn from Deut. 32:9, where it is used of Israel as Yahweh's special people, is assured.

This short pericope makes a distinctive contribution to the main purpose of the letter. It not only is calculated to inspire the readers with confidence that God's plan will not miscarry en route to its finale; it demonstrates to Gentile believers how they—with Israel's remnant—are part and parcel of the new people which has inseparable roots in the Israel of the old covenant.

Ephesians 1:15–23
Intercession for the Churches

In this section, thanksgiving (v. 16) merges into intercession (v. 18), with the uniting theme "The Church on Its Pauline Foundation." The characteristic title for the new Christian society is the body of Christ (v. 23). This designation of the church goes back to I Cor. 12:12–26 and Rom. 12:4–5. Most modern scholars, however, see a new dimension in Ephesians. The Pauline teaching is mainly expressed in functional terms: the church is like a body to carry out the tasks that Christ appoints for it, and in that instrument of service each member plays a part as a limb or member. This idea is present also in our letter (see 4:7, 16), but there is equally present a new idea: the church complements Christ the head and is given a status that some interpreters call ontological (v. 23). For Ephesians, Christ and the church are inseparable, though we may hasten to qualify this by the remark that there is no confusion of identity and the head remains firmly in control. Verse 23, at any rate, is an exegetical crux; we have no complete certainty as to its original meaning, even if some interpretations seem to us to be more plausible than others.

The earlier part of 1:15–23 is clearer. As a sign that the letter had a wider appeal than to the church in metropolitan Ephesus, verse 15 notes that the author does not know his readers personally. In this respect they are like the Colossians (Col. 1:3–4; 2:1). The news of their faith in Christ and its expression in active love to their fellow believers has reached the author at a distance. Here we have almost undeniable evidence that the letter was originally drafted and sent out as a circular document; the textual problems in verse 15, which center on whether "and your love" is to be omitted (so P46) or retained (most MSS.), do not alter the case.

Paul is known to have sustained a devoted ministry of prayer for his congregations, both those groups he knew personally (I Thess. 1:2–3; Phil. 1:3) and those familiar to him only at a distance (Rom. 1:9; Col. 1:3). What is novel here is the way the full content of such prayers is detailed. Also unusual in this example of apostolic praying is the manner in which the petition for illumination (vv. 17-18) shades off into a magnificent theological statement (vv. 20–23). The latter celebrates God's purpose in the resurrection and exaltation of Christ as the church's Lord and head. The writing is involved; in effect, it is one long, complex Greek sentence and suggests its origin in a liturgical setting. Later liturgies, such as the *Apostolic Tradition* of Hippolytus (ca. 215 C.E.), give illustrations of this kind of elevated prose, where prayer and theological confession mingle.

The intercessory elements in 1:15–18 used terms evidently drawn from the vocabulary of the Asian churches, and it may be also the language used in the debate between Paulinists and

21

their rivals. Examples are "knowledge" *(gnōsis)*, "wisdom" *(sophia)*, and "revelation" *(apokalypsis)*—all destined to figure prominently in the developed Gnostic systems of the late second century. Here the terms are boldly taken over and disinfected by being pressed into the service of Paul's gospel. Earlier (II Cor. 4:4–6, e.g.), Paul had employed this kind of revelatory idiom to stress how in Christ, who is the divine image, the embodiment of God was set forth. Now the prayer is that these readers may be given the insight to see the truth as Paul had expounded it and to remain firm in a time when rival teachers would sidetrack them (4:14; 5:6). The climax of the prayer picks up the term "inheritance," previously mentioned in 1:14, just as "the hope to which he has called you" will be brought back into the discussion at 4:4. Words for power (in v. 19) are piled up in an impressive, if bewildering, array. Indeed, an English translation is almost impossible with so many synonyms closely bunched together. F. F. Bruce asks, Why this attempt to exhaust the resources of language to convey something of the greatness of God's power? Because, he replies, the text is thinking of one supreme occasion when that power was exerted.

That supreme occasion is undoubtedly the raising of Jesus from the dead, seen in verse 20 as the signal display of divine power. Our understanding—and proclamation—of the resurrection should find a clue here. The New Testament writers invariably place the emphasis on God's action leading to the new age of messianic triumph rather than on Jesus' own emergence to new life. "He was raised" more than "he rose" is the way of expressing the mystery which is not the reanimation of a corpse but the taking up of Jesus' humanity into God's eternal purposes in a "spiritual body" (I Cor. 15:44–49; Phil. 3:21). Yet even this "event" at the turning point of the ages does not tell the whole story in the eschatological Great Reversal (Phil. 2:6–11). The raising of the crucified Jesus was followed by his elevation to God's "right hand in the heavenly places" (v. 20) where he is said to be seated. The picture language is taken from Ps. 110:1, a text that gave the early Christians their confidence to believe in the enthronement of Christ as a partner of the divine throne.

The development of this text beyond the early Paul (in Rom. 8:34) and into the later theological analysis offered in Hebrews and Revelation lies in the inclusion of Christ's dominion over all cosmic powers and his exercising a control that extends into the coming age (v. 21). There is little interest in the intervening Parousia which for Ephesians hardly comes into the picture at all. Instead, the victory of Christ, both present and future, is celebrated as a *fait accompli*. Not much hint is given here of the tension, so familiar from Paul, between the "already" and the "not yet." Our epistle sees the present elevation and the future kingdom as collapsed into a single reality, where I Cor. 15:24–25 keeps them distinct. Here is a problem caused by the presence of a bold assertion (in v. 22) that proclaims a realized eschatology and downplays the future hope. Some explanation is called for.

One suggestion, noting that verses 20–23 are composed in a style that is hymnic and that exults in Christ's exaltation, is that in its hymns the worshiping community greets the total victory as an already accomplished fact and brings the future into the present as a liturgical reality. A second proposal finds this confident assertion, that already God has given Christ head over all things for the church (v. 22), to be explained by a polemical purpose. The key is in "all things," that is, those demonic forces which militate against Christ's Lordship. They are firmly put in their place as under that Lordship and subject to Christ's control (contrast Heb. 2:6–8). Given the contextual setting of this chapter with its eye on those who were disputing God's sovereign plan, these verses offer an assurance that there is no part of the created order which is capable of effectively and finally thwarting the divine purpose, since Christ the head of the universe has already been installed in place. This is a "heady" assertion which the preacher and Christian advocate has to handle with some care. Some theologians remind us how near this confidence in the church comes to triumphalism, whether ecclesiastical or evangelical. We dare not overlook the mystery of iniquity and the powers of evil still at work in this age, and there is need to retain the future hope that only the Parousia may disclose. Perhaps the twin elements of realized eschatology and a yet unfulfilled future need to be held in equipoise, if not equilibrium. An older writer, John Baillie, is worth a hearing:

> Christianity must always maintain a realized and a futurist eschatology in balance. . . . In neglecting the latter it either shuts its eyes to the tragic realities of our continuing warfare or, alternatively, harbours utopian illusions of the possibility of their disappearance from the earthly scene. But in neglect-

23

ing the former it is failing to understand the specific character, the promise and opportunities, of the years of grace. (P.
207)

The church as Christ's body (v. 23) is the natural complement to Christ as "head," perhaps in the sense of "ruler" as if
to emphasize the thought of his control of all powers. "The
fullness of him who fills everything in every way" (NIV) is a line
to send us to the academic commentaries for further explanation. At issue is how to construe "who fills." Is it Christ who fills
the church? Or the church that fills Christ as his extension and
completion? Or is it Christ who is being fulfilled by the Father?
I do not think the text can mean that Christ is incomplete
without the church. Conclusive evidence in favor of the first
option—that is, the church is being filled by Christ—is given
by Stig Hanson (see Bibliography), though J. A. T. Robinson's
argument for the third possibility (see Bibliography) is worth
considering.

The Church's Story—
Past, Present, and Future

EPHESIANS 2:1–10

The passage 2:1–10 takes a broad sweep in its survey. It first
covers the plight of human life outside Christ and untouched by
the influence of his message (vv. 1–3), as it rehearses the ways
of living the readers knew prior to their entry into the Christian
society. From that point (in v. 4) it goes on to celebrate Christ's
coming by stating the great changes that have occurred in the
human condition because of God's initiative and action in grace.
The section up to verse 10 is really a placing side by side of two
contrasting panels. The first panel is verses 1–3: the previous
state of the readers; the second is verses 4–10: the new life in
Christ which has become theirs. The hinge is at verse 4a: "But
24   God, who is rich in mercy." The second panel covers not only
the present but the future of the readers as well. That future
prospect is found in verse 7. Here the thought reaches out to

"the coming ages" as the destiny of the church in the purpose of God is unfolded. The theme will be enlarged in chapter 3, notably at 3:9–11.

The connection of 2:1 with the foregoing chapter is not easy to see. The Greek verse has no main verb, and the initial phrase (in the accusative), "You were dead through the trespasses and sins," is left dangling until it is picked up and built into the syntax of verse 5 where part of it is repeated: "when we were dead through our trespasses." This break in the writer's thought suggests that the intervening verses (1*b*–4) are a digression that prepares for the triumphant announcement of the steps God has taken to meet the human condition, that of a person as a sinner whether as a Gentile (vv. 1–2) or as a Jew (v. 3). To accomplish this preparation the verb that best goes with the object in verse 1 is held back until verse 5; but in translation we need to supply it, as most modern translators do.

In another way, however, we can detect a line of continuity uniting the two chapters in our epistle. Earlier the author had praised God's great power in raising his Son from death's domain to a new place of authority. Now he proceeds to show that it is the same great power that is at work in vivifying the spiritually dead and raising them to new heights of life in Christ and with Christ. The thought is parallel with Rom. 6:1–11.

Ephesians 2:1–3
Humanity Outside Christ

Utilizing the proposal that the section falls into two main divisions, we may look first at the plight of the erstwhile pagans (and Jews) set out in verses 1–3. The root cause of the problem which Paul's gospel addressed is alienation which is depicted under the caption of death (as in Col. 2:13; cf. Rom. 5:21; 6:23; 7:11, 13). As in Pauline theology, sin and death are closely linked (Rom. 8:10; I Cor. 15:56). More detail, however, is given in describing the way the demonic powers held sway. Paul had already touched on this theme in Gal. 1:4; 4:3; II Cor. 4:4. Now the sorry condition of those who were the victims of superstition and bad religion in Hellenistic society—as the author would view their pre-Christian religious experience—is portrayed in a series of descriptive terms, all drawn from the Hebraic tradition. "The course of this world" (lit., "the age of this world") suggests that human life is seen under the malign influence of celestial powers thought to rule the universe, akin to "the elemental spirits" of Col. 2:8, 20.

"The prince of the power of the air" is a title for the devil (Eph. 6:11, 12), described as the ruler of demonic agencies in the upper regions of the sky (in ancient thought). In the cosmology of the Hellenistic age the interstellar space, especially between the moon and the earth, was believed to be the place of constant demonic activity, with baneful effects on all earth dwellers. The English word "lunacy" is derived from the Latin *luna* (= the moon) and should serve to remind us that we can no longer attribute mental and psychological disorders to such prescientific ideas, however much we may want to assert the reality of evil in society and human experience.

"The spirit that is now at work" could very well be an allusion to the evil effects of humanity's alienation from the true God as seen in human opposition to the gospel as Paul preached it. That opposition is motivated by the same malevolence that Jewish thought attributed to Satan's rebellion and downfall, that is, a refusal to obey God. Satan's rebellious spirit is still active in the people who have pitted themselves against God and God's cause (see for illustration II Cor. 11:13–15).

The sad fruit of this disobedience to God's gracious will for humankind is seen in the moral turpitude of society. Lists of vices as in Rom. 1:18–32 and Gal. 5:19–21 were commonplace among Hellenistic moral philosophers; and Paul will occasionally remind his readers of the way of life they have (or should have) left behind, for example, I Cor. 6:5–11. Only in the Ephesians text, however, is the precise wording found that men and women outside Christ (as in 4:17–19) are "by nature children of wrath, like everyone else" (NRSV). This is the literal rendering, which is only slightly improved in the NIV: "by nature objects of wrath." The idiom is drawn from the Old Testament and means "deserving of God's judicial condemnation." In the history of exegesis and Christian doctrine the phrase has played a significant—if wrongly conceived—role. It has been used to support a teaching on original guilt (as distinct from original sin, which says that all are born with a tendency to wrongdoing, not as actual sinners needing baptism to cancel out their inherited birth sin). And it has from time to time given rise to the false characterization of God as "angry" (cf. Jonathan Edwards's famous sermon title, "Sinners in the Hands of an Angry God"), which is a lamentably sub-Christian attributing of human emotions of vindictiveness and rage to God. What the phrase *does* say is that all are under divine judgment by reason of the moral choices they have made and that these in turn are dictated by their warped nature. Moral accountability is at the heart of the Christian understanding of the human condition and must never be compromised.

Ephesians 2:4–6
Humanity in Christ

The darkness of hopelessness (an idea given out in 2:12) and desperate need serves only as a backcloth to make the love and grace of God shine more brightly. God's character is essentially that of love (as 1:4 has also declared). God is "rich in mercy"—an Old Testament phrase to offset the mention of his wrath (see Ps. 145:8; Hab. 3:2). The evidence of God's loving concern which does not leave humankind to perish is seen in a twofold action. God has *both* made alive the spiritually dead (meeting the problem posed in v. 1) *and* has raised up those who were held down by servitude arising from their alienation from God. In effect, God has done for Christians what God has already done for Christ (1:20; see our comment on 4:21–24). This is one of the several illustrations that this epistle gives of the intimate bond uniting Christ and the church. The language here is rich in the use of verbs with the prefix "with" *(syn),* even to the extent that the author employs verbs like "he made us alive together with" which are not previously found in Greek literature and not attested again in later Christian writers (Bultmann, *TDNT,* 2:875).

The paragraph is unusual in having the perfect tense of the verb "to save" (in v. 5), and this is repeated in verse 8. Paul has either the simple past or the present tense marking the point in experience when believers came to faith and "were saved," that is, set free from sin's dominion (Rom. 8:24). The present tense (e.g., I Cor. 1:18) describes salvation as a continuing reality leading to its finale (see Rom. 5:10). By any reckoning, the

27

perfect tense—"have been saved"—is exceptional; it may be explained as a mark of non-Pauline theology which viewed salvation as an accomplished event, since the church is now seen as already raised to sit with Christ in the heavenly places. The forward-reaching aspect of salvation, so typical of Paul (as in Rom. 8:23–25), has been lost, subsumed under the conviction that the exaltation of Christ includes the present security of the church. Many argue that the eschatological tension in Paul has become relaxed in this letter and has dropped out of sight. But two points need to be kept in mind. First, "in the heavenly places" is the scene of conflict (6:12) as well as of peace and rest, and second, Heinrich Schlier defends the use of the perfect tense here as part of the letter's design to see the church's salvation in its total aspect, as something already fully achieved.

Ephesians 2:7–10
What It Means to Be a Christian

The future element is not totally neglected, however much the author wants to focus on God's completed salvation. The purpose of God's action in lifting the church out of the evil realm into Christ's heavenly presence is one that only the future—"the coming ages"—will disclose. This indebtedness to the Jewish time scheme of the two ages (II Esdras 7:50: "The Most High has made not one [age] but two") picks up what was said in 1:21 but gives it a new twist by adding that Christ's present enthronement extends into a future that will reveal more and more of God's grace to God's people. Once again the writer's stance is to explore the full range of divine activity-in-grace from what has been accomplished to what the future holds.

The entire process is God's doing—as II Cor. 5:18 insists—not humankind's; and it comes to us as a freely offered gift (Rom. 6:23). These verses have played a central role in both Lutheran and Reformed exegesis and have given to the church the slogans *sola gratia, sola fide* ("by grace alone," "by faith alone"). This is surely a correct understanding of Paul's mind, even if the little word "alone" derives from James 2:24! The rationale behind Paul's insistence, crisply stated by his loyal

28

follower, is that no person can be allowed room to contribute to his or her own salvation, else there would be ground "to boast." Bultmann (*TDNT,* 3:645–654) has helped us to see the importance of "boasting" which is more than proud assertiveness. It stands as a synonym of confidence in one's native prowess or spiritual competence (cf. Ps. 97:7 and Isa. 42:17, where boasting in idols is the same as trusting in them). The attitude represents the exact opposite of self-distrust, which casts itself on God and trusts only in God's mercy (Phil. 3:3–11).

After such a strong statement of human inability to help oneself, it is remarkable to come to verse 10, which praises the place of "good works." But these are not the "works" of verse 9; rather, they are the necessary consequence and outcome of the readers' new life in Christ. In the post-Pauline situation already foreshadowed in Rom. 6:1–12 and made explicit in the pastoral letters (e.g., Titus 2:14; 3:14; I Tim. 5:10), it looks as though Paul's absolutist stress on salvation by grace without works had become distorted and travestied. The righteousness of living and the high moral tone that Paul had also insisted on were overlooked on the mistaken assumption that Christians can live carelessly, claiming that if they indulge their desires and appetites, such lapses only give the grace of God more room for display. So the Pauline theologian in our letter has to wage a defense of his master on two fronts. Against those who would bring back the Jewish claims to merit by works he boldly restates the emphasis on "by grace alone." Equally to be rejected is the undermining of morality by those who, as in later developed Gnosticism, taught that once the pure spirit is saved, the body is an irrelevance to religion and may be safely ignored or indulged. Hence the call: "We are his creation" (Gr. *poiēma;* akin to II Cor. 5:17) created in Christ for (*epi,* with a view to) good works; this was God's design from the beginning (1:4) and part of his eternal plan for which the Spirit was given as a sanctifying agent (1:11–14; 4:30).

To set this well-known passage in a context like the one we have proposed will give it extra depth and weight. Preachers will need to keep the balance, so delicately presented here. Examples of the innate human desire to contribute to one's own salvation by various methods, including pious exercises of religion, are prevalent in every age.

Illustrations from the opposite extreme—attempts to treat salvation as a talisman and a passport to ethical indifference and

29

social unconcern—are powerfully present in the novels of John Updike. One of his characters speaks for this antinomian disregard: "Make no mistake. There is nothing but Christ for us. All the rest, all this decency and busyness, is nothing. It is Devil's work" (The Rev. Fritz Kruppenbach, in *Rabbit, Run* [New York: Alfred A. Knopf, 1973], p. 171).

The pericope 2:1–10 is a self-contained unit, dedicated to a single theme with its several facets. We can see this in the *inclusio,* or envelope style by which the readers' former life (v. 2: "you walked," i.e., lived) is set in contrast with their new life-style (v. 10: "that we should walk" in ways of goodness). Ephesians often seeks to point out this contrast of "before ... after" with the turning point of God's grace as the hinge. This kind of ethical maxim (once you were this, now you are that) will be developed in 4:17–32.

The Unity of the Church

EPHESIANS 2:11–22

A new section, with a new theme, begins at verse 11. This paragraph forms an extended exposition of the topic of the church's essential oneness in spite of the barriers of race and culture which kept apart Jews and Gentiles (i.e., non-Jewish nations in antiquity). The animosity that arose from fierce national identity was mutual. The Jews were despised as an odd-ball people, addicted to such strange customs as circumcision, Sabbath observance, and food laws that, for instance, forbade the eating of pork. Their worship of a single deity and their veneration of Moses' law as unique did not endear them to the Greco-Roman world of religious pluralism and tolerance. On the other side, reverence for Torah became a mark of Jewish self-consciousness which quickly turned to national pride (see Baruch 4:4) and a despising of other nations as benighted and outside the pale. So the battle lines were drawn, and "the dividing wall of hostility" referred to in verse 14 is no exaggeration.

To this sad situation the Christian message came as one of peacemaking and unity, and it built on attempts already in the

30

air as philosophers such as Epictetus were beginning to teach that human society could no longer afford to remain divided. The image of the body—one entity composed of several distinct but interrelated parts—was emerging at the time of the New Testament writers. It was Paul's major contribution to religious development to make this teaching the central, organizing principle of his missionary and pastoral ministry. The kernel of Paul's argument may be found already in I Cor. 12:13; Gal. 3:28; and Col. 3:11. What is singular and impressive about the passage in Ephesians is the way the earlier discussions are filled out. Where Paul had seen the Mosaic law as fulfilled (Rom. 10:4) or set aside (II Cor. 3), the language of verse 15 talks of the law's being canceled and done away with completely. Another unusual emphasis here is the way the church takes the place of national groups in verse 15 ("one new person in place of the two") instead of merely existing alongside the ethnic divisions that persist (as in I Cor. 10:32). One explanation for these new elements in stating and illustrating the church's oneness as God's creation may be a reflection of a development that followed after 70 C.E. when the temple at Jerusalem fell and Judaism suffered a traumatic blow (hence v. 14 is often taken to refer to the dividing wall in the temple court). Another reason may be the author's use of liturgical language drawn from a baptismal hymnic setting. The language of liturgy tends to state Christian realities in a triumphant manner; hence the creation of a new society is celebrated, but more as an ideal and a goal to be attained than a present fact of experience.

Before commenting on the individual parts of this section, we should note what lies at the center of the argument. This is in verse 14: "he is our peace, who has made us both one." As a programmatic statement, this sentence combines within itself elements taken from the surrounding verses. We may tabulate these: (1) The enmity between Jews and Gentiles has now been overcome and pacified; (2) the disparate segments of the divided first-century world are now called to a harmonious amity within the fellowship of the Christian church; and (3) both Jews and Gentiles in losing their ethnic and racial claims gain something in return which is said to be far better, namely, a place in Christ's body, as Christ's body, thereby forming a new race of humanity. Later writers therefore call the church "the third race"—neither Jews nor Gentiles but Christians. And, promises this text, Christians also gain an unsurpassed privilege of access

31

to God, which they could never have known in its depth in their previous and unreconciled state.

No passage of the New Testament could be more relevant to the closing decades of the twentieth century than this magnificent statement of the one hope for our race. The world that we know and inhabit is fallen, divided, suspicious, and full of the possibility and threat of self-destruction. The apostle's teaching holds out the hope and prospect of a reconciled, unified, and amicable society, whose microcosm is seen in the church's worldwide, transnational, and reconciling family.

Three main affirmations are made in 2:11–22, to which we shall now turn. Within those verses the exegetical problems in verses 14–18 are considerable and center on whether an original text containing a baptismal statement has been taken over and enriched by the Pauline author. The reason to suspect that it has been lies in the cumbersome nature of verse 15, a feature that the RSV smooths out in concern for clarity. Interested readers may consult the present author's chapter in *Reconciliation* (see Bibliography on Colossians). It has tried to disentangle the two layers of tradition and redaction in an endeavor to get to the heart of the letter's teaching on reconciliation, a term that in the New Testament carries several different—yet interrelated—meanings, namely, personal, ethnic, cosmic, and missionary.

Ephesians 2:11–13
The Gentiles
Before and After Christ's Coming

This section recalls that the first readers were Gentile believers in Asia Minor; as such, they are bidden to reflect on what their religious condition in pre-Christian days looked like from a Jewish viewpoint. They were classed by the Jews as "uncircumcised," thus standing outside God's covenant with Israel. The phrase "in the flesh" is not the typical Pauline idiom for the power of evil in human experience. Here its use is ironical and refers to the act of circumcising. Paul is more interested in the religious significance claimed for the Jewish rite (Rom. 2:25–29) and can show his disdain (Phil. 3:3), while concentrating on the spiritual or inner meaning (Gal. 6:15; I Cor. 7:19) in line with Israel's prophets such as Jeremiah who called for circumcision of the heart (Jer. 4:4).

What was the state of the non-Jews as seen here? A three-fold reply shows that (1) they lacked any hope in a Messiah. Indeed, Messiah's coming in the intertestamental *Psalms of Solomon* about 50 B.C.E. meant the destruction of the Gentiles. (2) They suffered a deprivation in that they did not have the right of citizenship within the elect nation. This is the sense of "alienated from the commonwealth of Israel," and its meaning is confirmed in verse 19. (3) The saddest of all misfortunes is described in the wording of verse 12c: "having no hope and without God in the world." The two parts of this description go together and need to be understood carefully. "Without God" does not mean a denial of God's existence. There were very few atheists (in the modern sense) in the ancient world. Rather, the thought is that men and women outside the Judeo-Christian revelation (or the church, our author would insist) lack a true knowledge of God. The uncertainty arising from a pantheon of many gods and goddesses coupled with a prevailing tendency to despair (as Gilbert Murray noted in his phrase "failure of nerve," used of Hellenistic society; see Bibliography) led to a sad state of hopelessness. The Christian answer to both problems is found in a knowledge of the true God whose Son has opened a new era for the Gentiles in every age.

That new eon is one whose characteristic is access to God, according to verse 13. This is a central theme in Ephesians and has a contemporary relevance, since it poses a perennial issue. Verses 13 and 18 are linked with word association, thus enclosing a self-contained pericope by the device of *inclusio.* The contrast "far away . . . brought near" is borrowed from the language of Isa. 57:19 in the LXX and was used by the rabbis to denote the respective stations occupied by the nations of the world and Israel (see the idea in Ps. 147:20; 148:14). In the Christian adaptation of this idea the framework is borrowed but filled with a novel interpretation. Access to God is now freely available to all, irrespective of their previous racial and religious impediment. "In Christ," that is, Israel's Messiah and through his sacrifice on the cross, the nonprivileged Gentiles have come to share with Israel in the covenant of fellowship with God. What remains to be explained in detail is how this transforma-

33

tion should impact on relations between Christians of both origins within the church.

Ephesians 2:14–18
Jews and Gentiles
Are Now One Body in Christ

Among the titles carried by "Messiah" in the Old Testament a key one was "Prince of Peace" (Isa. 9:6). *Shālōm* means much more than absence of hostility, like an armed truce or "cold war"; it connotes well-being and security at every level. For Pauline theology, "peace" carries two main ideas: reconciliation to God ushers us into a new relationship with God known as peace (Rom. 5:1); and in this paragraph a second dimension is added, namely, the reconciliation that unites men and women across a cultural and religious divide. Both groups, formerly alienated from each other by reason of fierce nationalism, cultural pride, and religious claim, are united to become "one." That unity finds its locus in the place they now take in God's family as God's new humanity (note v. 14). The barrier that divided is broken down, and access to God previously a bone of contention between Gentiles and Jews is declared to stand open to all races. Moreover, the access works on a new plane, since it now betokens the horizontal communication that Christ makes possible. Cultures and classes that had been separated by walls of prejudice and tradition are now opened to one another, and the lines of connection and conversation are established. It is this twofold imagery of a double reconciliation—to God and to our fellow human beings—that is the unique contribution of Ephesians and marks it out as one of the most timely New Testament documents for our day.

There are, of course, difficult exegetical problems the preacher will need to ponder in approaching this section. Thankfully they should not inhibit our confidence that this message of reconciliation is one of God's surest words to our troubled society and fractured world. Take the matter of "the wall" (v. 14; NIV, "barrier"). Obviously the metaphor speaks of separation and alienation, as when Winston Churchill in his early

34

postwar speech referred to an "iron curtain" coming down to separate the countries in eastern Europe extending from Stettin on the Baltic Sea to Trieste on the Adriatic and their western neighbors, or when we recall the once infamous Berlin Wall. Is there, however, a more exact allusion in mind?

The commonest illustration of the imagery is in the temple balustrade which separated the Court of Gentiles and the Court of Women in the Jerusalem temple. This fence with its warning inscription ("No man of another race is to enter within the fence and enclosure around the temple") served to remind the non-Jews that they must keep their distance from Israel's sacred shrine (for example see Acts 21:27–31). That barrier, verse 14 declares, has been broken down in the sense that access to God is no longer restricted to Jews and their cultic observance.

Martin Dibelius, however, asks a question of this interpretation: Would the Gentile readers in Asia have understood this allusion? Doubting this, he proposed that the background reference is to Gnostic images of a wall that was believed to separate the cosmic aeons and divide the heavenly *plērōma* from the earthly region. According to this view, the allusion is to the Gnostic redeemer's reentry from the terrestrial zone (to which he descended on his mission from the heavenly world) to the celestial sphere. He has gone back to his upper world, and his flight path (to use the modern expression) necessitated the breaking down of all hindrances that stood in his way en route from "below" to "above." This piece of cosmic movement was taken by the second-century Gnostics to be a symbol of the way humanity's access to the heavenly regions was prepared as the ascending savior broke open the way as forerunner. Against this view, F. F. Bruce offers the telling criticism by observing that the barrier in the biblical text is a vertical one denoting a division between two groups of people in this world rather than a horizontal division between upper and lower spheres. And, we may add, the verb "broken down" (NRSV) refers more naturally to a fence standing vertically.

A third possibility now may be considered, which the present writer has suggested elsewhere (see *Reconciliation,* chap. 9; see Bibliography on Colossians). The wall that set up hostility is a covert allusion to the Mosaic law and its scribal interpretation. As explained in the *Letter to Aristeas* (a Jewish second century B.C.E. document), the intention in God's granting the law to Israel was to protect the nation from the Gentiles and so

35

indirectly to prevent the Gentiles from having access to God because of Israel's particularism. Hence the Gentiles were said to be "afar" from both Israel and God's covenant (v. 13). What kept them at a distance was Torah thought of as summed up in its "commandments and regulations" which both defined Israel's covenant status and made it impossible for non-Jews to enter. The verb "broken down" speaks to that need in the sense of abrogate and abolish (thereby going beyond Rom. 10:4). Torah's role had to be drastically rethought in the post-Pauline Gentile age if the notion and acceptance of a universal church was ever to gain credibility and appeal. Once more the letter blazes a trail that was at the same time necessary and risk-laden. It was necessary, because only a type of Christianity that was more than a revamped Judaism could survive as a world religion. Yet it was risky because the overthrow of Torah's authority marked the first step on a slippery road to antinomianism which rejected all moral restraints. The Gospel of Matthew with its bid to reestablish a nomistic basis for faith and ethics (albeit as Messiah's law: see Matt. 5:17–20) shows a reaction to the risks embodied in the law-free charter of our letter. The church, it has to be confessed, is still wrestling with this tension, and its preachers have still to grasp the nettle of how to proclaim a faith cut free from legalistic requirements and restrictions while in the same breath offer some moral guidelines to safeguard ethical responsibility. To state the problem is much easier than to attempt a solution.

Up to this point (at v. 17) the writer's thought has lain in the past tense. He has dealt with God's action in breaking down obstacles to a worldwide reconciliation. Christ's death has introduced men and women to God; and by the same token he has done away with barriers that kept Jews and Gentiles in opposite and opposing camps. Hostility in both directions is happily at an end, and in its place is the accession of peace (v. 15), a much desired reality in Roman society ever since the emperor Augustus began his era with a much vaunted promise of global peace and security. Poets like Ovid and Virgil hailed its arrival, but it was short-lived, as names such as Nero will recall.

Now (at v. 18) a clinching item in the argument is introduced. Whether one finds the theological reasoning behind verses 14–17 to be persuasive or not, there can be no denying the appeal to experience in verse 18 and what follows. United in fellowship, Jews and Gentiles in Christ discover their oneness in a mutual and free access to God by the (Holy) Spirit who is the author of unity within the church, as Paul had taught (I Cor. 12:13).

Ephesians 2:19–22
The One Church on the One Foundation

The particle *ara oun* (NIV, "consequently"; NRSV, "so then") draws out a consequence from a previously established fact or conclusion (e.g., Rom. 5:18). Perhaps the author has a vivid, concrete expression of Christian community in mind, such as common table fellowship in which believing Jews and Gentiles met in celebration of the Lord's Supper. At this time, unlike the unhappy episodes of Paul's earlier ministry (e.g., Gal. 2:14–21), the Gentiles were in no way treated as inferior, nor was their admission to the church regarded as exceptional or a back door entry. Rather, they were welcomed as full members, "fellow citizens with the [Jewish] saints." Both classes constitute the members of God's household as a single entity, members of one society (4:25) with equal rights and privileges. This is the final statement of what Ephesians regards as the special emphasis of Paul's ministry (3:6).

The church as a building to house the family of God is one of the distinctive features of the letter's ecclesiology, along with the church as a body (1:23; 4:16) and a bride (5:25). Paul's teaching in I Cor. 3:10, 16 is here assumed and extended, with a nice exegetical conundrum thrown up along the way. If Christ is the building's foundation (I Cor. 3:11), how can verse 20 be reconciled with that Pauline assertion? Admittedly the Greek genitive is unclear and can be taken in several ways, even if we concur with the majority opinion that "apostles and prophets" are to be understood as Christian leaders. What is their relation to the church's foundation? Is the genitive one of possession (the church is erected on a foundation on which the apostles and prophets rest: so Anselm and Aquinas)? Is the foundation that laid by the apostles and prophets (genitive of origin: so NEB and GNB)? Or is the genitive one of explanation or apposition, that is, the foundation consists of the apostles and prophets, as many modern interpreters believe and JB renders, thereby setting this verse at odds with I Cor. 3:11?

Perhaps there is no great difference between the *ultimate*

37

meaning of the second and third views just outlined. It is difficult to separate Christ as the true foundation from those who
proclaim him, as Ernest Best notes: "If Apostles . . . were those
who laid foundations [cf. I Cor. 3:10; Rom. 15:20], it is a probable association of ideas to think of them as themselves the foundation stones" (*One Body in Christ,* p. 164). In other words, it
is the *proclaimed Christ* who is the basis of the new temple; and
in their activity of proclaiming, the apostles and prophets play
a unique role because it is their ministry that lays the foundation. Not that they are the foundation in their persons; rather,
they fulfill their role in the exercise of their function as official
bearers of the revelation of Christ. Heinrich Schlier (see Bibliography) in his comment on this verse may be quoted:

> The "preached" Christ cannot be separated from the apostle
> and his apostolate. There is no access to Christ other than
> through the apostles and prophets, who have preached him
> and who themselves become and remain in their preaching
> the foundation.

If we understand "apostles and prophets" to include both
their oral witness and their literary deposits in the New Testament Scriptures, this citation is exactly in line with the Lutheran and the Reformed teaching on *sola scriptura,*
Scripture's witness which "drives" *(treiben)* us to Christ.

What is remarkable, however, in this passage is the way
there is one group that is involved with the church's foundation:
apostles-prophets (the single definite article before apostles
governs the second noun in the pair). It suggests that our understanding of "apostle" may need to be enlarged. Ordinarily we
classify such persons as either the original followers of Jesus
according to Acts 1 or representatives or delegates like Epaph-
roditus (in Phil. 2:25–30) whose work was patterned on the
Jewish model of the synagogue messengers. A third category,
however, is offered in Ephesians, embodied in Paul, who combined in one person *both* the role of witness to the "mystery of
Christ" (3:5–6) along with the "original apostles" like the
Twelve, *and* the prophetic-teaching office of those set apart to
declare God's word to the nations (Rom. 1:1, 5; 11:13).

The church rests on a single foundation in the sense that,
as the "cornerstone" in ancient building methods had an importance as the stone used by the architect-builder to determine
the "lie" of the whole building, so Jesus Christ is the pattern by

38

which the church is being shaped by God. Its growth is set by its conformity to this original plan. Yet "church growth" in verses 21–22 is given a meaning not currently associated with that slogan. It is not measured by statistics or budgets. Rather, it is the growth of a living organism which takes shape by the Spirit's guidance through the circumstances of history and in a fashion drawn from the erection of Solomon's temple (I Kings 6—8). The church is invested with a sacred aura as the dwelling place that God desires to inhabit. But it is no temple made by human hands, as a material structure might be; it is a spiritual body composed of men and women in whom God's Spirit lives (I Cor. 3:16). The Qumran community looked forward to a new temple to supersede the cult at Jerusalem with its rites and rituals. That hope was amply fulfilled in Christ's new people, both Jews and Gentiles, where God finds his habitation and whose lives express to the world the ultimate worship of God in terms of dedicated service and the liturgy of everyday living (Rom. 12:1–2, 4, 9–21).

Paul's Apostolate And His Prayer for the Church

EPHESIANS 3:1–21

Paul's calling to be "an apostle of Christ Jesus by the will of God" (II Cor. 1:1) was foundational to his role as church planter and leader (Rom. 11:13; 15:15–21). He never seems to have wavered in this conviction that stemmed directly from his knowledge of the risen Lord (I Cor. 15:9–10). Yet much of his pastoral correspondence is taken up with a defense of this very issue, and he is constantly engaged in polemics against those who would cast aspersion on his apostolic standing and authority (a major theme in II Corinthians, but it runs also through Philippians and Thessalonians).

After Paul's lifetime the same spirited defense, but on fresh grounds, was made by his disciples. In the section covered by chapter 3 (esp. 3:1–13) we have to ask ourselves whether these statements on behalf of Paul's apostolate read more naturally as his own spoken claims to be Christ's representative to the Gentiles or whether we are listening to the call made in Paul's interests after his death by some admiring follower writing "out of love for Paul" (amore Pauli, to use Tertullian's later phrase)? In other words, this chapter poses the questions of the authorship and purpose of the epistle in an acute form. We are bidden to come to some decision about the autobiographical posture the author adopts in these paragraphs. Is the material best understood as coming from Paul himself or from a later admirer reflecting on the significance of his apostolate? Exegesis too will be affected by such a decision, and preaching themes will be governed by some prior consideration of the point these highly personalized discussions are meant to serve.

The autobiography, in fact, merges at verse 9 into a statement of the content of Paul's preaching in the light of the special destiny he was charged to fulfill (vv. 3–6). The important statement in verses 5–11—on either interpretation of who the precise author may have been—is given for the effect of showing that Paul's apostolic ministry to the Gentiles is based on the place it holds in the economy of God's saving purpose for the world through the churches founded by Paul.

The personal element creeps in again as an interlude (vv. 7–8) or parenthesis set within the larger apologia. It is resumed at verse 14, as the author offers a memorable pastoral prayer, in Paul's name, for Christian congregations in the world, embracing heavenly and earthly dimensions (vv. 14–19). This concludes with an equally notable doxological ascription of praise (vv. 20–21).

The saying that reminds us that as a person prays, so that person's beliefs come to light (lex orandi, lex credendi) is a sound one and is richly illustrated by this concluding section.

Ephesians 3:1–6
Paul's Calling and How He Understood It

40

Paul's personal name is intended to give emphasis to the prayer that will follow (vv. 14–21); it also is evidently added to assert Paul's ownership of the claim that is registered on his behalf. In fact, there is no matching verb in verse 1 to follow his name, and the verb is held back until verse 13, which introduces the prayer. Likewise the mention of him as "a prisoner of/for Christ Jesus" is not a piece of self-advertisement but a reminder of his credentials as apostle on behalf of the Gentiles (a similar bid to establish the integrity of the Pauline mission is seen in II Tim. 2:9–10).

Paul is unknown to the addressees (see 1:15)—which reads strangely if this letter is primarily directed to the church in metropolitan Ephesus where Paul spent several years, according to Acts 19:10; 20:31. Nevertheless it is now a matter of record that his Gentile ministry is widely known and ought to be acknowledged as authoritative. It was a ministry that claimed as its origin divine revelation (v. 3, a claim going back to Gal. 1:11–12) and as its substance the inclusion of the Gentiles in a multiracial church where ethnic and religious barriers are transcended (2:14, 17-18). This reality is dubbed "the mystery of Christ" (1:9). The conviction here registered by some post-Pauline group is that only the apostolic preachers of the Pauline churches have grasped the insight that first came to the great apostle, and it is *their* claim (made in the phrase "holy apostles and prophets," v. 5) that they stand in succession to those preachers on whom now they confer the aura of sanctity in the title "holy." The latter term does not relate to any personal virtue or distinction; it is simply the author's way of paying veneration to the immediate entourage of Paul, among whom we may name Timothy and Titus, whose mantle has passed on to the writer's generation (a more exact way of locating the author's ambience could be to see him mirrored in II Tim. 2:2). Verse 6 is a noble tribute to the quintessence of Paul's gospel and its fruit in the emergence of a Gentile-oriented congregation. The messianic promise, formerly regarded as Jewish privilege (1:13) and from which the Gentiles as non-Jews were excluded (2:12, 19), is now widened to embrace all peoples. The richness of their inheritance, lauded profusely in 1:18, is spelled out in a triad of terms, linked by assonance with the same prefix (Gr. *syn*): the Gentile believers in Messiah Jesus are coheirs, comembers of one body (4:4), and cosharers of the (messianic) promise that reached back to Abraham (Gen. 12:1–3, which Paul exegetes in a universalistic manner in Gal. 3:6–9, 14, 29). 41

Ephesians 3:7–13
Paul's Calling and How He Fulfilled It

Mention of Paul's "gospel," lifted from Gal. 3:8: "The scripture, foreseeing that God would justify the Gentiles by faith, declared the gospel beforehand to Abraham," sets the writer on a track that involves an extolling of Paul's career qualifications and an indirect defense of what that career entailed (v. 13). Evidently Paul's apostolate, known to be pockmarked by suffering and eventual martyrdom, was under fire, and the author rallies to his side by this reopening of his file and retelling his life story. But the essential praise is really reserved for Paul's message which, reinforced by divine energy and given consequent approbation (v. 7), centered in an ethnic and cosmic reconciliation that was God's saving plan from the beginning (v. 11). Yet apostle and message belong together, with a third inextricable component the church whose role is to be the agent through which this proclamation is not only made known but also embodied for all to see (v. 10).

This summary statement is an attempt to draw out the main thrust of verses 7–13. Yet we have skated over several exegetical questions. Paul's self-depreciatory tone in verse 8 is expressed in language that almost defies translation. He confesses to his own inadequacy and weakness as a foil to extol the greatness of divine power (cf. 1:19); his self-denigration is that of a servant (Gr. *diakonos*), who is "lower than the lowest of all God's people," as the literal rendering runs. This bold remark is in line with the tradition (in Acts 8:1; 9:1; Gal. 1:13, 23; Phil. 3:6 and later to be formulated in I Tim. 1:13) to the effect that the historic Paul was known as an arch-persecutor of the church; yet he was marvelously won over and captured for the service of the one he attacked. He is praised as the exponent of "the unsearchable riches of Christ," which is tied in with his role as apostle to the Gentiles. His task is seen as enlightening all peoples by the process of unveiling God's redemptive plan, once concealed (3:5) but now brought into the light. This is the mystery (1:9, 17); and the Pauline churches, true to his spirit, are summoned to be witnesses to it and at the same time to be its vehicle to the nations.

The good news is addressed primarily to men and women. Yet there is another dimension to it, expressed in verses 9–10, in a passage that poses several conundrums. The dimension takes in a nonhuman, cosmically oriented realm of angelic and demonic intelligences, known as "the rulers and authorities" set in the heavenly places (NRSV, here and at 6:12). These spiritual agencies, generally accepted as real forces in Hellenistic culture, are said to receive the news of Christ's victory that leads to their submission (Phil. 2:9–11; Col. 2:15). The divine enterprise, then, that vindicated Christ's Lordship at the resurrection, celebrated in 1:20, brought an end to the malign regime of these spirits and their tyranny over human life in the shape of fate and astrological fear (see on 1:21–22). Later (in 6:12) it will be conceded that the church on earth has still to do battle with these powers which continue to exert their influence. They are thought of here, however, as already subjugated in "the eternal purpose of God" because to them God's wisdom in Christ's cross displays his "manifold [lit., many-colored] wisdom," to dazzle them by its sheer simplicity and apparent weakness. The passage is evidently in debt to Paul's exposition in I Cor. 2:6–10; 15:20–28. There the tension between what is already achieved at the resurrection and the future and final conquest of evil powers is at the heart of the Pauline eschatology. The items that are noteworthy in Ephesians are the stress of the former aspect (but not to the complete exclusion of the second) and the role of the church as the locus of divine power which impresses the cosmic forces. Paul's apologia in II Corinthians 10—13 of strength-in-weakness is given a theologizing twist in celebration of all that the victory of Christ has already secured (cf. II Cor. 13:4) in terms of the way the dualism of God versus the powers is overcome. Thus heaven and earth are brought together in reconciliation, even if the ultimate restoration lies yet in the future and the present warfare of 6:12 is still menacing.

These verses are full of language, concepts, and imagery that are difficult to hold together in a realistic manner and still more troublesome to preach. They savor of a first-century worldview not shared by our technological and empirical age. Yet they do speak to a basic human situation, provided we lay hold of the master theme, namely, the announcement that in the church which lives on the far side of the Easter vindication there is no reason to fear those alien forces of fate and determinism which haunted the Greco-Roman world and still retain their grip on our society. At verse 12 the scene switches to the church set in the real world. The readers are reminded that they enjoy "boldness and confidence" for living as twin necessities to challenge any dualistic worldview or idea that we are at the mercy of impersonal cosmic forces. So this piece of writing has an eminently practical intent; and from the celebration of Christ's supraterrestrial triumph the assurance of personal fellowship with God is deduced. As in 2:18, the chief element in the dramatic presentation is that no hostile power can separate the church—or the world—from the Father, since both human and cosmic destiny are disclosed in Christ (1:10). A recent author, Clinton E. Arnold, puts it like this: the epistle "is a response to the felt needs of the common people within the churches of western Asia Minor, who perceived themselves as oppressed by the demonic realm" (p. 171). There is therefore no reason for the readers to "lose heart." Rather, they should take courage from their initial acquaintance with and response to Paul's message and not doubt it.

Ephesians 3:14–21
Paul's Prayer for the Church

Mention in verse 12 of "access," an interesting term to denote an introduction to someone of august presence, such as a Hellenistic king or ruler, prompts the rehearsal of a Pauline prayer. Fittingly it is addressed to the Father (1:2, 3, 17) who is made known in his Son and whose "fatherhood" sets the pattern for all family life, both among the saints in heaven and the church on earth. This conjunction is a further token that heaven and earth are now joined together. God as Parent is the archetype of this reality, while the appellation still has a resonance of intimacy and approachability found in the Aramaic prayer speech of *Abba* (Rom. 8:15; Gal. 4:6), "dear father."

The content of the petition is twofold. The apostle prays for the Gentile audience, as the posture and the prayer look back to verse 1, that it may be strengthened in its inner life by the Spirit who is the bond uniting all believers, both Jewish and Gentile (4:3–4). The complement of this request is an invoking of the indwelling Christ who comes to make his home in the church (v. 17 goes back to 2:22 which has the same Greek word usage). The combined effect of this double petition is seen in a result which, in spite of mixed metaphors and some hyperbolic language, is designed with a practical end in view, that is, that God's power may be seen at work in the church in which God's fullness dwells by the presence of Christ and the Spirit (1:23; 2:22; 3:17). The assortment of metaphors—"rooted" is horticultural, denoting a firm bed in which plants are set; "grounded" borrows the idiom of architecture (as in 2:20) and ensures a strong base on which a superstructure rests and rises—is easily disentangled, though it is clearer in Col. 2:7. Less comprehensible is a set of terms taken from the intellectual and moral universe (v. 18). "Knowledge" is most properly exercised regarding God's redemptive plan in all its scope (the spatial terms have a parallel in some magical texts where they denote the extent of divine power, as in Rom. 8:39, and became popular in later Gnostic speculation to describe the dimensions of the divine). "Love" lies at the heart of God's nature and purpose in this epistle (see 1:4–6; 2:4; 5:2, 25; 6:23), and human love in the church answers to it (1:15; 5:28; 6:24).

It is appropriate that in the sublime doxology (vv. 20–21), God's presence-in-power should be located both in Christ (cf. Col. 2:2–3) and in the church, since the church is intimately associated with him (1:23; 4:15–16; 5:30). For the Paul of Ephesians, Christ and his congregation are not two separate entities but are so closely conjoined that it would be permissible to write of one corporate whole, Christ-in-his-church. Indeed, that is exactly the genius of this epistle's ecclesiology.

The New Humanity in Earthly Relationships

EPHESIANS 4:1—6:20

A distinct break in the author's writing comes at 4:1. At this point the direction of the address changes. So far in the letter to Gentile congregations the theme has been that of the way in which God's purpose was conceived and executed, and the

45

prevailing mood has been one of praise and thankfulness. In a sentence, the reason for praise is that believers have been brought from death to life, and both Jewish and Gentile Christians now form one, single church. Further, this "plan" of God (as 1:10 calls it) or "mystery" (to use the term in 3:4–6) to have one people corresponding to one head, Christ, was realized through Paul's mission and ministry, which is gratefully recalled—though the plan stretched back to God's eternal counsel (1:4, 11; 3:9). The author looks back on the accomplishment of that task as he recalls Paul's historical ministry and his place in the history of salvation (3:1, 7–19). By this token we may account for the appeal to Paul's name in 3:1 and the closing off of the passage in a eulogistic ascription of "glory to God" (3:20–21).

Yet the ideal of the first part of the letter needed down-to-earth application to the churches standing on the Pauline foundation. How far they would have understood and appreciated the fulsome language and breath-catching idioms of chapters 1—3 is hard to tell. So, self-consciously—denoted by the repetition of the phrase "I . . . a prisoner for the Lord" (4:1, matching 3:1)—the writer now turns to a practical outworking of the ideal in everyday living. The technical term is "paraenesis," that is, moral exhortation and admonition or, as A. M. Hunter puts it, "moral instruction with a dash of exhortation" (p. 52).

More simply, from the rarefied heights of "the heavenly places" (lit., "the heavenlies," 1:20; 2:6) the thought comes down to the earthlies of daily experience and communal living in the Greco-Roman society in which the Pauline churches were set. The author is placing before his readers and hearers the guidelines of Christian conduct and deportment in the church and the world. The foundation has been laid in a magnificent exposition of the theme, Christ-in-his-church; now the structure must be erected, with its complementary theme, the church-in-Christ or, more properly, Christ's church in its relations with society.

The division of the document into these two segments—forming a diptych, a double-facing panel—helps our understanding. It is important for us to keep the order straight in our thinking. First, there is the theological side of the writer's ecclesiology (1:3—3:21) as he views the church under the aspect of God's eternal, far-reaching purpose. Then comes the application in a set of principles that are to govern the church's life in the world (4:1—6:20); it is ecclesiology brought down to earth—grounded in some harsh realities and facing acute pastoral and ethical problems. Yet the author's confidence is undimmed that those who have shared his convictions so far will take seriously their vocation as it is to be worked out in everyday issues.

Before the author gets into specific concerns, he must first give an overall picture of what that vocation is to be. This is the particular interest of 4:1–16, a section that functions like a hinge to connect the two halves of the diptych (literally so: chaps. 1—3 and 4—6 of the letter). Put another way, 4:1–16 acts as a frontispiece to the balance of the document. Because this section is a key one, it is important for us to see how it is programmatic of what is to come. Based on what has preceded it, 4:1–16 announces in five bold strokes what the author believes about the churches as they confront the society around them. Let us set down these points and elaborate them as we move into the succeeding chapters. They express a summary of the items to be looked for in what follows.

1. With the announcement of "the calling" to which they are summoned, using a favorite expression of Paul's (Phil. 3:14; Rom. 1:7: "saints by calling"; I Thess. 2:12: "lead a life worthy of God, who calls you into his own kingdom and glory"), he sets the stage. The calling to the readers is to be true to their destiny in the light of their place within the church which by definition is unity (4:2–6).

2. Yet unity does not mean a monochrome, deadpan uniformity, which might be the case if the church were a thing, an inert and static object.

3. Rather, the church is an organism, pulsating with life and made up of living persons who are responsible for growth of character and personal development, according as they use the gifts that Christ has bestowed (4:7).

4. Christ's purpose is that church members shall reach maturity (4:13). With that end in view, he has prepared and bestowed gifts to be exercised by his people (4:8–12).

5. The church's progress is marked by a growth out of infancy into maturity as it takes on the character of Christ who is head (4:14–16). The growth of the body is set within the Pauline framework of "upbuilding" (another of Paul's favorite terms: I Cor. 12—14) in love.

47

Ephesians 4:1–6
The Church's Vocation in the Light of Its Unity

The author uses the apostle's summons to the Colossians (Col. 1:10) to lead a life that pleases God as "worthy of the Lord." He is also indebted to the earlier letter for the moral qualities he lists (Col. 3:12–13). Indeed, from Gal. 5:22–23 we see the force of Schleiermacher's dictum that "the fruits of the Spirit are the virtues of Jesus." What is exceptional here is the way the qualities of humility (a tricky word to define) and gentleness are completed by the encouragement given to "make every effort to preserve the unity the Spirit makes possible," a thought that looks on to verse 4. So the unity is a divine gift, but it must be cultivated and cherished as Christians live together in harmonious relationships. Such unity is "made fast with bonds of peace" (NEB) forged by Christ's reconciling work (2:15–18).

In a series of creedlike formulations the meaning of unity of the Spirit is unpacked. Note the repeated (seven times) emphasis on the term "one"; and there are three sets of pairs, forming a triad of couplets. We can display this diagrammatically:

one body (=the church)—one Lord (the church's head)

one Spirit (by which Christ is confessed)—one faith (I Cor. 12:3)

one hope (accepted in baptism)—one baptism (I Cor. 12:13)

After this trinity of unities, the creedal statement is sealed with a reference to "one God"—a monotheism that Christians share with Israel (I Cor. 8:6)—who is known in his self-revelation as the Father "over all" in creation, as Son "through all" (the preposition is one of mediation, as in 2:18), and as Spirit who is "in all" the family of God.

The allusion to baptism suggests that this is an early Christian baptismal credo enshrining the chief elements of a confession of faith made in the rite of initiation. If so, the force of the appeal is to invoke what Christians share as their common heritage in the faith: one God (Deut. 6:4), one Lord (the original New Testament creed: Rom. 10:9; I Cor. 12:3), and one baptism of the Spirit by which all were engrafted into the body (I Cor. 12:13). We may call this a rudimentary trinitarian faith, though it is still undeveloped and not yet elaborated as in the classical creeds. But its simplicity is its strength, and it may be the focal point of ecumenical unity for which modern Christendom still is searching. When Christians come together across the dividing fences of their denominational allegiances they find they have more in common than they suspected. They meet not to create unity but to confess it.

Ephesians 4:7–12
Christ's Gift and His Gifts

The commentators explain this intricate passage in various ways. The heading we have chosen reveals a preference for and relies on the insights of G. B. Caird in a discussion unfortunately tucked away in a hard-to-reach place (see Bibliography). The issue turns on the meaning given to "the measure of Christ's gift" (v. 7), a term that runs in tandem with "grace" in the same verse. All agree that "grace" *(charis)* here does not mean what it does in 2:6, 8, but it is the author's equivalent of Paul's word *charisma* in Rom. 12:3–12 and I Cor. 12:4–11. So our author faithfully reproduces Paul's teaching on needed spiritual gifts to ensure that each person plays his or her part in the life of the body, the church. He returns to that inclusive conviction in verse 16: "the whole body . . . grows effectively according to the due measure of each separate part." Note that the section verses 7–16 is framed by the same link term, rendered "measure" *(metron)*. So the writer's carefully crafted section is inclusive in a double way: literarily he uses the device of *inclusio,* and theologically he wants everyone to be included in the scope of the gifts that were Christ's endowment at his enthronement.

But what of "Christ's gift"? The verb "was given" in the (punctiliar) aorist tense looks back to a particular occasion and to that time when the gift was made. The latter is best taken as

49

referring to Pentecost, when the exalted Lord gave his gift (singular) to the church. This is the gift par excellence, namely, the Holy Spirit, as the Fourth Gospel comments (John 7:39; 20:22; see Acts 2:33). Now we run into a problem. Ascent and descent are brought together in an involved way, and the illustration is not helped by the fact that the Old Testament text of Ps. 68:18 does not agree with the version cited by Ephesians; in fact, it says almost the opposite. The Hebrew psalmist wrote of the king who, when victorious over his foes, *received* gifts as tribute, a sense found also in the Septuagint. True, Jewish interpretations (found in the Syriac Peshitta and Aramaic Targums) have the verb "to give," and it is likely that the author is drawing on a current Aramaic paraphrase and changing it as well, since the Targum relates the text to Moses who gave the law to men. Our passage has the ascension in view, but what on earth does "he . . . descended into the lower parts of the earth" mean? Is it Christ's first coming to this world in the incarnation (so NEB)? Or is it a descent to the underworld after his death (as in Rom. 10:7; I Peter 3:18–21; Rev. 1:18)? This latter is in the margin of the New English Bible.

Here Caird helps by offering a third possible interpretation. The "descent" is in fact a veiled allusion to Christ's coming in the person of the Holy Spirit at Pentecost. Already Paul had conjoined the exalted Lord and the Spirit (II Cor. 3:17); now this disciple of Paul dramatizes the identity by saying that Christ returned when the Spirit came; it was in this way that Psalm 68 was fulfilled, for the present Christ-in-the-Spirit is the one who gave both his Spirit and the gifts of the Spirit to furnish the church with all needful ministries.

To see the various options, we may schematize them as shown in the diagram. In this diagram, (i) represents the "descent" of 4:9–10 and (ii) stands for the "ascent," with broken lines, indicating movements not explicitly mentioned in the text. Note that in model III, which we have followed, ascent comes before descent chronologically; this fits the sequence once we recognize that the adverb "first" (v. 9, KJV) is omitted in the best textual readings and evidently was added by later copyists. It is definitely not implied. By using Psalm 68 (a Pentecostal psalm in Jewish liturgy: see Kirby) the author is emphasizing Christ's victory in his return to the Father and his subsequent bestowal of gifts as he came back to earth in the person of the Spirit.

MODELS

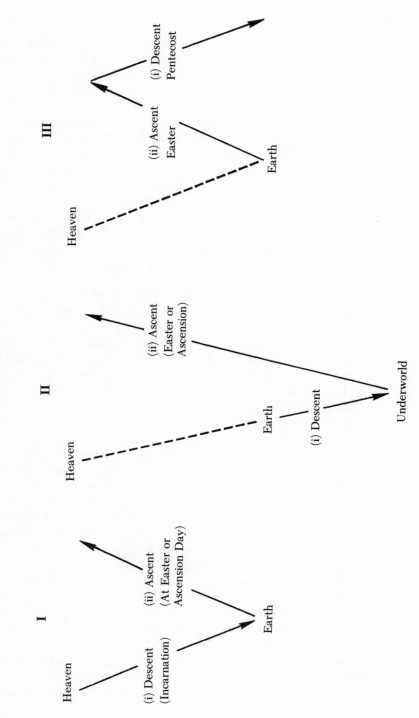

The gifts are listed in verses 11–12. Apostles and prophets hold first place (as in I Cor. 12:28; *Didache* 11:3). The reason given for their importance carries forward Paul's teaching, as we noted at 2:20. These are the leaders of the early church whose primary function was witness to the risen Lord; they were human vehicles to express his mind to the congregation, though their authority could be challenged, as it was at Corinth (I Cor. 14:29, 37; cf. *Didache* 11:4–12). Evangelists were people like Philip (Acts 21:8) and Timothy (II Tim. 4:5), charged with the task of proclaiming the good news.

"Pastors and teachers" go together, linked by one definite article. This suggests two functions undertaken by the same person, whose task is described in Acts 20:28. They were evidently local congregational leaders, otherwise known as "elders" (Acts 20:17; see I Tim. 4:14; 5:17 for their role in some congregations also claiming Pauline foundation).

Verses 12–13 can be puzzling. What is intended, however, is clear enough, namely, that Christ's gifts of various ministries are designed to benefit the entire body of Christ. The "saints" means all Christians, and "we all" are to attain that maturity which is described as nothing less than reaching the stature of Christ in his fullness (v. 13). There is then an interplay of a regular ministry, ordained and appointed by the head of the church, and the rank and file of members, which leads to the desired goal. That is, the end in view is the building up of the body. Verse 16 reverts to this final result.

The tangle of the Greek in verses 12, 16 permits at least two options. According to the one, the ministers mentioned in verse 11 are enablers whose job is to equip God's people so that the latter in turn may fulfill *their* work of ministry and so build up the body. This is a popular view today, enforcing the democratic nature of the church in which all the members are called ministers, some "ordained" but all with shared ministry.

The rival view also sees "the equipping [or perfecting] of the saints" as the main responsibility of the ministers who are Christ's gift, but the work of ministry belongs particularly to those special leaders and it is they who are to build up Christ's body. This, it is held by those who propound it (e.g., Hanson; Masson), is an exegetical conclusion based on the text, though it can be pushed to an extreme in maintaining that this view makes the apostolic ministry a necessary part of the church's ongoing life. Some scholars point to this understanding of an

52

indispensable ministry as part of the developed structure and organizational pattern of church and ministry found in such writers as I Clement (96 C.E.) and Ignatius (ca. 110 C.E.).

Perhaps we are not driven to that far-reaching conclusion. Rather, we should see a line of development from the free, unstructured patterns of church authority at Corinth to a situation in Asia Minor that this letter addresses. Circumstances, which will be described in verse 14, were threatening these congregations. The author makes his plea for resistance to such pressures and puts in his appeal for cohesion and support for Paul's teaching by insisting that the apostolic ministries do serve as a bulwark and safeguard. We shall return to this discussion at verse 16, which is often neglected when the meaning of verse 12 is sought.

Ephesians 4:13–16
The Church's Path to Maturity

"Building up the body of Christ" (v. 12) is the grand design for which God in Christ gave both the Spirit (the gift, v. 7) and the Spirit's gifts, that is, the persons listed in verse 11. There is an end in view, so that growth, the master theme of this short section, may at length attain its goal. The writer finds paradox useful to expound the faith and uses it here. "Unity" is *both* what we already have, since it is the work of the Spirit (4:3–4: we must keep what we have!), *and* the future aim toward which we must work. The same paradox is seen in verses 13, 15 which is part of the transformed eschatology of Ephesians. "The church grows toward Christ; it does not expect him to come to it," as hope of an imminent Parousia would suggest (Masson). Whether the growth is physical (as in the current slogan of "church growth") or in quality is not clear. The latter is more likely correct, given that "knowledge of the Son of God" and the "upbuilding in love" speak more of the development and enrichment of Christian understanding and character than of statistical increase.

The threatened dangers behind the scenes in verse 14 are not further specified, unlike Col. 2:13–19, where some particular aberrant Christology and indulgence in ecstatic visions lead

53

to the need to hold fast to the church's head. The Ephesians writer will later go into some detail about the trouble afflicting his churches; here he is content to enter a warning plea and condemn the false trends in advance. His pastoral concern is to accent the need for growing up out of infanthood into maturity, a growing up that is qualified as being "growth into [Gr. *eis,* suggesting movement] Christ" and as being rooted in "the truth," that is, the gospel according to Paul, presently under fire in his region. Because serious issues are at stake—one may speak of a landslide away from the Pauline tradition in Asia as a factor in the background throughout this letter (see II Tim. 1:15 for a hint of evidence)—the author appeals to the apostolic ministry, epitomized in Paul's mission (2:20; 3:1–13), as a stout bulwark to defend the church. From Col. 2:19 he borrows the medical idioms used in verse 16 (especially the word rendered "joint," Gr. *haphē,* as in the phrase "joined and knit together by every joint with which it is supplied") to stress the need for healthy growth. To be sure, every part of the body is called to play its role under the supervision of the head, which is Christ. But we must add the middle term "joint" to the equation: Christ the head = his body, the church. It is through "every joint" (or ligament or connection) that the entire body is compacted and unified; and each part is supplied with a connecting joint.

The link in thought with verses 11–12 is clear. The exalted Lord, runs the argument, works to control, to unify, and to use the various parts of his body through his gifts of ministers. It is they (apparently) who act as Christ's messengers to direct the body and so prepare all God's people to engage in his service. To bring about the upbuilding of the body—"upbuilding" and "body" are two terms that belong to the same world of metaphor—the head and each part must cooperate. To enable "each part" to work as it should, the intermediary "joints" play a vital role in the analogy. This may appear at first glance as a mechanistic arrangement: Christ → his ministers → the church's members. The growth of the church thus seems to depend on the ministry. Yet this conclusion (marking an advance on Paul's ecclesiology, and no doubt tailored to meet the pressing needs in the Asian churches of a later decade) is tempered—but not altered—by several factors. These are *(a)* the reminder that the ministers are Christ's gift to the church, not authority figures in their own right (v. 11); *(b)* the caution that they also are "under his control" (v. 16) and are themselves part of

54

the body, not separate from it or placed over it; and *(c)* the wording of verse 16*b:* "the whole body grows and builds itself up *through love"* (GNB). Love—extolled in I Corinthians 13 and to be applied in the author's forthcoming section of 5:25–33 to Christ and the church as a model for human relationships—is known in Paul's thought as that attitude and action which casts aside self-promotion and seeks the well-being of others (I Cor. 8:1).

Ephesians 4:17–32
A Statement of the Christian's Social Conduct

In recent days scholars have devoted a great deal of attention to the ethical teaching of the New Testament. This is part of an inquiry that seeks to explicate and illustrate the nature of the Christian life as the New Testament authors understood and stated it. Preachers also face the same difficult task in relating their present-day messages to the needs of their people in the light of what the New Testament contains, and they should be aware of the twin dangers that lurk. One is that of trying to prescribe detailed rules and regulations to cover all contingencies of moral behavior. Those who seek to avoid this danger will need to ask whether it is adequate to have the section in Eph. 4:17–32 described as "Rules for the New Life" (as in NRSV summary added to the text). After all, there is nothing in the New Testament moral teaching resembling the Old Testament book of Leviticus! To be sure, the call to holy living resounds through both testaments, but is the basis of that call the same? Second, the presentation of New Testament morality as though it were moralism is a pitfall to be avoided. We are not true to the church's commitment to revelation in the New Testament when we reduce the message to a tame acceptance of moral truisms like "Be neighborly," "Do your best," "Be patriotic." We all need the reminder that Christian ethics begins with the resurrection of Christ, and imperatives (do this, don't do that) are grounded in the indicatives of what God in Christ has done for the world and is doing by sending his Spirit into the human

55

scene. Yet we are still groping for more help, even when it is said epigrammatically that what the New Testament gives is not directions but direction. How can that direction toward the fullness of Christian living be understood and applied? Two discussions (Bultmann, *Theology*, 1:105–106; Dahl, chap. 2) will aid us considerably and provide the entree we need to our passage. They join to offer five principles that run through the ethical sections of the epistles.

1. "Once this was hidden, now it is revealed" (Rom. 16:25–26; I Cor. 2:7–8; Col. 1:26–27; Eph. 3:4–5, 9–10) is a phrase that picks up the way God's saving plan, once covered in obscurity or known only in part (in the Old Testament), is now—in the new age of messianic fulfillment—made known. Believers are invited to live in its light (see Eph. 5:8–17) by appreciating the offer and responding to the demand of the new period of human history into which they have been ushered by Christ's coming. When Germans neatly express this by talking of *Gabe* (gift) leading to *Aufgabe* (requirement), it helps us to see the intimate link, provided we remember to keep the sequence right.

2. When the scheme of revelation just mentioned is applied to human conduct it becomes, "Once you were this, but now you are that." The contrasting adverbs ("once . . . now") are the key, as the New Testament writers begin by describing what the converts were like in their old life as a foil to make clear the realities and glories of the new existence in Christ. There are examples of this contrast in Gal. 4:8–9; Rom. 6:17–22; 7:5–6; 11:30–31; and I Cor. 6:9–11, but the best illustrations come in our present passage, as we shall see.

3. "Conformity to Christ" is often appealed to as a motive for Christian living, with several variations seen in Rom. 15:3–4, 7–8; II Cor. 8:9; Eph. 5:2, 25, 29; cf. Eph. 4:32; Col. 3:13.

4. What has been termed a teleological motif is seen in statements that open with a declaration of all that Christ has done for the church and then glide into an implicit call for believers to accept the benefits he secured for them. His action was purposeful, and they are bidden to accept and live by the purpose for which he called them.

5. Lastly, there is the hortatory motif, using such verbs as "I beseech," "entreat," "exhort," and such injunctions—which are better described as appeals, since the imperious tone is muted—are reinforced by accompanying phrases such as "in

the Lord" or "in the name of the Lord" to supply an authority base. This is a typically Pauline mannerism (I Thess. 4:1; 5:1; Rom. 15:30; I Cor. 1:10; II Cor. 10:1; Philem. 9, 10), and we observe it in Eph. 4:17.

This survey does not exhaust the types of ethical appeal, but it will be enough to alert us to what we should look for in the opening of Eph. 4:17. Two principles or axioms are pressed into service: the "once . . . but now," which we may label the out-working of a new relationship; and the idea of "put off . . . put on," based on the contrast of the two natures and with a decisive turning from the old and a glad embracing of the new nature. This is a shift of allegiance that is rooted in the baptismal experience (cf. Gal. 3:27 which shows how the actions relate to taking off clothes and putting on new garments in the rite).

Patterns of Old and New Life Contrasted

In this section 4:17–32 it is the moral state of the Asian congregations that brings these principles just discussed into play. Formerly the readers adopted the only way of life they knew, namely, the pagan outlook and practices whose colors are darkly painted in verses 17–19. At conversion they exchanged—for many of them, like the Corinthians (I Cor. 6:9–11) in a dramatic renunciation—these evil ways and took on a new deportment that vitally affected their character and manners. Verses 28–32 recall the change with an insistent summons not to relapse into former ways. Whether they were being misled into thinking that moral issues were of little consequence once the spirit was enlightened, as Gnostic religion taught, we cannot say for certain. But there are signs in the letter (5:6: "Let no one deceive you") that such was the case.

The other appeal, "put off . . . put on," comes at verses 22–24, where a general statement is made to do with the two sides of our personhood, represented by the old life (or "self," NIV; Paul's teaching on the *sarx*, "flesh," in Gal. 5:13–26 is similar) and the new way of life (or "new self," NIV; the contrast in Gal. 5 with the *pneuma*, "Spirit," runs parallel). So this summons is close to the Pauline injunctions to "walk by the Spirit, and do not gratify the desires of the flesh," meaning our selfish nature, akin to what the apostle learned from his Jewish upbringing when he contrasted the two propensities, good and evil, which strive to control pious Jews. The teaching here, however, is set in the more dramatic context of baptism.

57

"Life in the old Adam" is one way of expressing the types of behavior to be shed. For those in the Pauline school (Paul himself, the tradition in our letter, I Peter) there was a favorite expression to sum up in a nutshell the two orders of existence: in Adam/in Christ (e.g., Rom. 5:12–21; I Cor. 15:22, 44–49). The key lies in the preposition "in" which may be taken in several ways, starting with Albert Schweitzer's proposal to see the term as expressing a physical state, that is, believers are "physically interdependent in the same corporeality" of the exalted Christ. Almost certainly this is a mistaken idea, since it blurs the personal element in the faith-union with Christ which Paul regarded as central. C. F. D. Moule (pp. 60–63) has a good discussion of other possibilities of what "being-in-Christ" means before concluding (rightly, in my view) that the preposition is to be construed of a place, but metaphorically and yet realistically. Above all, the term is a corporate one. The risen Lord is the "corporate representative" of his people who share in union with him both the benefits of his cross and victory and the obligation to be the new people of God of which he is head.

If we add to this three other considerations, we are well on the way to getting "inside" the rather obscure train of thought in 4:17–32 in the light of the explicit baptismal language used and the practice referred to in 5:14. First, if "in Christ" is a societal term, we should expect "in Adam" to be the natural counterpart. Being a Christian means transferring allegiance from the old order. That order is being in "Adam" (as Adam = humankind's representative in biblical and rabbinic anthropology to stand for humanity's idealized past, its present fallenness, and its future promise). The new order is in "Christ" who typifies the re-created society as a microcosm of renewed humanity. Second, the transition point where this transference was made was baptism whose descriptive terminology is seen in such contrasting terms as *(a)* put off/put on; *(b)* darkness/light; and *(c)* death/life, along with ideas such as the sealing of the Spirit (4:30). All these terms have baptismal association. Finally, most interpreters see a baptismal hymn, with its three-line invocation in 5:14, introduced by a citation formula. It is said:

58

Awake, O sleeper,
And get up from among the dead;
And Christ's light will shine on you!

A good way to communicate the train of thought in 4:17–32 is to see it as moving from what we were in Adam to what we are (and should become) in Christ. The transition goes back to the contrast "formerly . . . but now" principle mentioned above. We may call it the outworking of a new relationship, with verses 22–24 functioning as the hinge on which the ethical admonition turns. The point may be illustrated in the aspiration which most of our hearers feel that they should be better people:

> And ah for a man to arise in me,
> That the man I am may cease to be!
> Tennyson, *Maud*

"Life in Adam" is depicted in some bold strokes (4:17–19). Then follows a short paragraph in which the readers' acquaintance with the Christian message is assumed (4:20–21a) with its implied call to quit the old life under sentence of decay and death and embark in a new way which, it is promised, is a renovation restoring us to Adam's first glory through union with the last Adam. Baptismal profession is in the foreground of this hortatory appeal, as readers are recalled to what they learned in catechism and training. The point is made: become in reality what in your baptism you professed to be. But in the background is the christological component akin to Rom. 6:1–14. Their baptism into Christ replicated in experience all that Christ himself underwent. He died to sin; in him they died too. He was buried; they join him in the act of baptism. He was raised to new life; they likewise are called to "walk in newness of life" (Rom. 6:4). If this parallelism is intended here, it gives extra force to an exegesis of 4:21–22, proposed by C. A. Anderson Scott (p. 36), that really illumines the puzzling phrase "as the truth is in Jesus." He wants to render the Greek as an adverbial expression, meaning "as in truth it was so." Let me paraphrase: You heard the Christian message and understood the teaching that—as it really happened in the case of Jesus who (first) put off the old self in his baptism (= his death on the cross) and became the new Adam at the resurrection—so you too are to abandon old ways and take your place in the new Adam.

Having stated the overall principle, we may set down how the axiom of "formerly . . . but now" is applied in concrete situations. Some adaptation of apostolic analysis and instruction will be needful to make this section come alive for modern congregations, though parts of it are surprisingly relevant as

59

they stand. We suggest a threefold approach, corresponding to the areas the text mentions.

1. Once ignorant as pagans, they are now enlightened with the true knowledge of God (vv. 17–19). The central terms in this indictment, which should be compared with Rom. 1:28–32, are "futility of their mind" (the Greek word *mataiotēs* recurs in several places in the New Testament, suggesting that vanity or illusion has cosmic ramifications [Rom. 8:20], is connected with idolatry [Acts 14:15], and issues in a way of life that has lost touch with reality [I Peter 1:18]). The lexical partner is "insensitivity" which can refer to a spiritual condition that borders on indifference and leads to a way of life where all distinctions between good and bad, wholesome and destructive, are lost in a willful disregard of moral values. There is an insatiable quality about this sad condition if we follow the NIV rendering: "with a continual lust for more," but it is more likely that "greed" *(pleonexia)* adds a third term, whether it is avarice (somewhat out of place here) or, rather, unrestrained appetite (as in Col. 3:5).

The gospel's response is to offer the true knowledge of God leading to an intellectual awakening and moral awareness (as in John 17:3; Gal. 4:8-9; I Thess. 1:9; Acts 17:22–31)—both parts of the renewal of the mind promised and expected in 4:23.

2. Once dead in sins (Eph. 2:1) and as pagans unhappily cut off from God (4:18), they are now forgiven (4:32), raised to new life (2:4–10), and are presently alive to God with a nature and outlook like his (4:24).

Living in the network of new social relationships, as being-in-Christ, entails some down-to-earth behavior patterns, spelled out in 4:25–31. The patterns include love of truth; honest purpose in daily work, with an altruistic concern for others in need; sincere speech which has no truck with falsehood, anger, gossip, or rotten talk; and a recognition that we are not our own because of the Spirit's "seal"—a mark of ownership and protection in biblical religion and contemporary business practice. These features sum up the application made. They represent what George Johnston calls "the character of the New Adam" and bear out the point that the teaching is set in social context.

A couple of well-known verses deserve extra comment. "Be angry but do not sin; do not let the sun go down on your anger" (v. 26) is now proverbial—but often misunderstood. First, a technical matter. In the spoken and written Greek of the day (the koine) the imperative mood expresses not only a command but also a requirement or a concession. So the meaning is: You may be angry . . . if you can't help it, but do not sin thereby. It is intended that anger should not become an obsession and nursed to the point of resulting in a fixation. Hence the allusion to the sun not going down on the day's unguarded moments.

Speech is much in evidence, for words are the index of a person's character (Matt. 12:34). Good words are greatly to be sought for, to encourage the growth of other people (v. 29), "as there is need" (NRSV) or "according to their needs" (NIV) or even "if you have a good tale [Gr. *chreia,* a term for an illustrative story in literary criticism] to tell." Words that "bring a blessing" (NEB) should be our aim—in conversation, in social intercourse, and in Christian fellowship (5:19, 20).

3. Once under the regime of the old self (4:22), they are now glad to shed this dominion and accept a new control, the new nature (4:24). The twin parts of the new order of existence are given in the latter verse: *righteousness* (lost in Adam, now regained in Christ as part of the process of "rightwising" or justification that reinstates sinners in communion with the creator God whose own nature is righteous, i.e., salvation bringing; but here the ethical implication is to the fore) and *holiness* (a term picked up at 5:3, where the "holy ones" are expected to be true to their name) that stem from truth. Both terms are to be understood—and proclaimed in our sermons—under the rubric of God's Lordship which both sets the standard and supplies the motive power for attaining that norm in daily and communal living.

"Enemies of the soul" may be a caption under which we can tackle this section, for teaching or preaching purposes. They are identified as ignorance, death, and bondage. The gospel comes as good news—yet note that (as E. P. Sanders has taught us) apostolic thought moves from solution to plight—against such a backcloth; and because inevitably the setting is dark and somber the good news shines more brightly with its promise of light dispelling the darkness of these age-old enemies which our society and we face. Knowledge, life, and freedom are accents of the authentic Pauline word; the contrast is epitomized in 5:8, a paraenetic tag that sums up this section:

61

Once you were [in] darkness, now you are light.
Live as children of light!

Ephesians 5:1–20
Christian Conduct Illustrated

The Christian life in section 5:1–20 is shown to possess a distinctive ethos and pattern. It is set forth in a way intended to be both a challenge to contemporary society and a rebuke of it. We may note, however, that no mandate is offered for Christians to withdraw from the world as though they were ascetics or fanatics. The moral guidelines which combine both situational and prescriptive elements—to use the convenient modern terms—are constructed on the implied assumption that it is possible to live the full Christian life in the context of "the world." Some necessary safeguards, however, are entered to counteract the seductions of those (in v. 6) who would "deceive" the readers. The call is sounded: "Do not associate with them" (v. 7) as a stern reminder that the Christian ethical ideals are always under fire, and the threat to accept a relaxed morality, possibly coming from gnosticizing fellow Christians whose presence and influence lie in the background of this letter, is a clear and present danger.

One way to meet the problem is to recall readers to their Christian status and vocation. The author does this by several methods.

First, he addresses his people, giving them titles and appellatives that have a moral kick in them. They are "children" of God (v. 1), called to imitate the Father's loving nature. What God has done and continues to do in the gift of Christ is an incentive to moral endeavor, since it reminds the church that it is a ransomed community, like old Israel, and summoned to reflect the holy character of the redeemer God (v. 2). In both testaments the distinctive name for those who are chosen to be a holy people is "saints," as in v. 3, a term that picks up Israel's destiny as both a nation set apart from other peoples (Ps. 147:20) and dedicated to divine purposes in the world as Yahweh's "treasure" (Exod. 19:5-6; Deut. 7:6; 14:2). Such a privilege is not achieved without cost, as the stories of the "saints of the Most

High" in Daniel illustrate. Suffering is part and parcel of this destiny, which lays a claim of high moral principles on God's people set in a hostile world.

Yet another title is "children of light" (vv. 8–14). This title is interesting not only for its association with the community of the Dead Sea scrolls who also used this description to set off their group from the surrounding "children of darkness" but for the example in verse 14 of a baptismal reminder. At the commencement of their new life as believers these men and women had been brought into the full light of Christ. We may overhear the very terms of their initiation in a three-line baptismal chant contained in verse 14:

> Awake, o sleeper,
> And get up from among the dead;
> And Christ's light will shine on you!

The life situation of this snatch of early hymnody is evidently baptism, which was frequently known in the church as a person's "enlightenment" and depicted as the rising of the new convert from the death of sin into union with the living Lord (Heb. 6:4; Rom. 6:4–12). The writer harks back to this experience as a reminder to his readers that they should now make good their baptismal profession by walking in Christ's light and stirring themselves to active witness. Romans 13:-11–14 makes the same point.

The appeal to wisdom in 5:15–18 marks out this section as indebted (if indirectly) to the sapiential tradition of the Old Testament. Israel's sages in Proverbs and Sirach sought to guide their contemporaries by recourse to a way of life patterned on wisdom, that is, obedience to God's law and loyalty to his cause in everyday circumstances. Terms like "wise," "foolish," and maybe "filled with the Spirit" indicate how this wisdom instruction may have entered Christian moral theology at an early stage. The point is that believers are cautioned not to wander aimlessly through life's maze or become victims of a moral stupor (hence v. 18a: "Do not get drunk with wine, for that is debauchery," leading to stupefaction). Rather, wisdom's call is to leave "dame Folly" (as in Prov. 5—7) and to follow the path of sobriety and seriousness, based on a conscious effort to ascertain the divine mind and to employ one's opportunities to best advantage (v. 16). The prudential element in this ethical admonition should not be overlooked or despised. People today need to have some ethical advice clearly spelled out for them and set down in manageable and easily understood terms.

The cameo of 5:19–20 is again of interest in allowing us to take a peep at the early churches in their worship practices. Hymnic praise has always conveyed the note of thanksgiving to God, which is par excellence the noblest use of the human voice (v. 4). When Augustine defined a hymn as "a song of praise to God" he had primarily in view certain of the Old Testament psalms and Christian compositions that celebrated God's creating and redeeming purposes in Christ. The latter creations, for example, the Te Deum, which tradition ascribes to Augustine's period, go back to New Testament precedents in Revelation 4—5 and to such memorable examples as Phil. 2:6–11; Col. 1:15–20; and John 1:1–18, all three notable hymns to Christ that announce his cosmic role and salvific mission in bringing heaven and earth together. They are essentially hymns devoted to the theme of reconciliation. "Spiritual songs" has the more general term, "odes," to suggest a range of Spirit-inspired pieces that operate on the horizontal plane as exhortations to one's fellow believers to spur them on in the journey of life. Hence the verb in verse 19 is "addressing one another." Augustine's definition is seen now to be too constricting. Our use of "words sung to music" in modern worship should make room for this third type of public utterance and give our fellow worshipers a chance to express their deep-felt feelings in a way somewhat more relevant to our hopes, fears, and struggles than traditional hymns perhaps allow. This is a much canvassed area of debate, and we are all self-appointed experts in the field of liturgical and corporate praise. "The best hymns are the ones I like" expresses an apparently irrefutable opinion, and wise pastors will make certain allowances to take in a wide variety of taste and religious experience.

Looking back on 5:1–20, I suggest that the text falls into three fairly well delimited areas. The overall rubric is the Christian church's self-identity which, says the author, must not be attenuated or compromised by listening to the siren calls of those who would adopt a lower set of standards (vv. 5–7). This advocacy of a clear-cut profile explains why the text has been constructed to set in opposition the church's way and the world's threat to that way. The three "contrasts of opposites"

64

are (1) love excluding lust (vv. 1–7); (2) light banishing darkness (vv. 8–14); and (3) wisdom correcting folly (vv. 15–20).

Lest this arrangement give the impression of a negative attitude toward Christian morality it should be also stated that the author's use of Pauline materials safeguards his position from being treated as a new legalism. A life enveloped and expressed by love, set out in verse 2, is a noble inspiration; and it is right to observe how, with all the lurid concentration on the evils of speech in verse 4, the characteristic note of thanksgiving is struck. A thankful disposition shows itself in more than one way. It is courtesy to our fellow human beings (v. 4) no less than the offering of praise and worship to God on high (v. 20). And once we compare the wording of verse 20 with the parallels in Col. 3:17, 23 we can see how such gratitude spills over to the whole of life's activity and turns worship into an everyday experience. George Herbert's lines are to the point:

> Teach me, my God and King,
>   In all things thee to see
> And what I do in anything
>   To do it as for thee.
>
> All may of thee partake,
>   Nothing can be so mean
> Which with this tincture, "For thy sake"
>   Will not grow bright and clean.
>
> A servant with this clause
>   Makes drudgery divine;
> Who sweeps a room as for thy laws
>   Makes that and the action fine.

Two remaining phrases stand out in this context and may be taken over as they stand by the modern interpreter and preacher-pastor. The first is contained in 5:15–16, the second in v. 17. In the first phrase (vv. 15–16) the author issues a call to wisdom that is set over against the folly of the surrounding pagan (i.e., non-Christian) environment. The path taken by wise people (v. 15) has to be understood on its Old Testament background. There wisdom is not so much an intellectual achievement as an attitude toward life. It begins with a knowledge of God and a steering away from all that displeases God (Job 28:28; Ps. 1; Prov. 4:5–9; 8:1–36). Wisdom also is described generally as a religious stance undertaken by godly persons in Israel and their response to situations of a problematic kind, for example,

65

occasions when evil is rampant, godless people prosper, and the righteous face unexplained trials. Wisdom is that outlook which enables a pious believer in Yahweh to face life, to make sense of its enigmas, and to surmount its problems. The last-mentioned item is specially highlighted in recent discussions of wisdom in Israelite life and faith. It picks up the seminal remark of W. Zimmerli (see Bibliography), who argues that wisdom permits the righteous not only to know life's secrets, pleasurable and painful, but to gain the mastery over them. This idea is given prominence in our text as well.

The practice of wisdom in everyday conduct set in a hostile society involves specific moral activities and choices. They are particularly mentioned in verse 16: first the zest for living that is always on the alert for opportunities to be turned to good account. The language of "making the most of the time" (NRSV) is borrowed directly from the commercial vocabulary of the marketplace (Gr. *agora*). The verb is *exagorazomenoi,* which means literally snapping up all chances of a bargain that are available. It refers here in part to the stewardship of time as God's priceless commodity. There is a call to invest our energies in occupations that are worthwhile.

Such a call as shown in verse 16 springs from the recognition that "the days are evil." This is a typical sentiment of Jewish wisdom writings, but it gains point when it reminds the reader that, for all the heavenly character of the church as raised to the glory of the exalted Lord (1:20–23; 2:6), it still lives in a world where evil powers are prevalent, as 6:11–12 will go on to stress.

The other moral claim that our author lays on his readers (the first was contained in vv. 15–16) is the summons to self-understanding (v. 17). It also belongs to the sapiential tradition of early Judaism, though it is equally shared with popular Hellenistic moral philosophy. The referent is the will of God, for it is as men and women live in the light of that purpose and in fellowship with God (II Tim. 2:7) that they discover the path to wise living. One certain way of disrupting that fellowship and refusing to accept God's will comes in a blurred vision which in turn is caused by an abandoning of self-control.

Verse 18 signals the danger of intoxication through which the vigilance of the moral censor is lifted and a gateway opened to immorality. The Christian's avoidance of profligate living (the NRSV renders "debauchery"; the word means any excess that leads to loss of self-control) was the occasion both of the amazement and of the hostility of pagan neighbors for whom carousing was part and parcel of the social conviviality (I Peter 4:4; II Peter 2:13). The warning "Do not get drunk with wine" is from Prov. 23:31 (LXX). It touched upon a very real peril confronting Christians in a pagan culture and is a timely admonition in every age.

In a daring contrast the next half-verse (18*b*) carries forward the idea of drinking to excess. Let the infilling you seek be that of the Spirit, not of wine. As "Be filled" is present tense, indicating a continuing experience, the thought may well be: As overindulgence in wine is a common occurrence in the world around you, so let the Spirit's fullness be your constant preoccupation. The test of such an experience follows in verses 19–20, which have the worship of the Christian assembly in view. The keynote is jubilant praise (v. 20) which is the church's corporate response to the goodness of God and forms a bridge that links the ethical teaching of the epistle so far to what follows.

Ephesians 5:21—6:4
Christ, the Church, and the Family

Mention of the church engaged in worship (5:19–20) invites a consideration of the place taken by women, first in a church service and then, as a natural sequel, in the domestic relationship with their husbands and families. Two preliminary issues need to be examined before we get to the details.

First, it is uncertain where the paragraph begins and whether 5:21 belongs to the preceding or the following discussion. In the NRSV the division comes after verse 21, but there are grounds for claiming that verse 21 acts like a bridge between what has gone before and what follows. The reason lies in the absence of a verb from the Greek of verse 22, which makes it unlikely that the author would begin a new section with no verb in the sentence! Clearly the verb must be carried over from verse 21, as in the NRSV, which inserts "Wives, be subject. . . ." The submission, then, of verse 21 looks back to the description given of the church at worship (vv. 19–20) and forward to the attitude of a woman to her spouse. If this is the case, the author may be easing his way into the latter discussion by

67

remarking in verse 22 that it is in services of public worship that a woman ought to be submissive to her husband, and he is drawing on traditional material in I Cor. 14:34 which uses the same verb and I Tim. 2:11 which has a cognate noun. The need to set Christian worship on a right basis is the starting point for his treatment of the analogy between Christ and the church. As a clinching observation that the unit is 5:21–33, with verse 21 functioning as a curtain raiser to the ensuing discussion, we may observe that "reverence for Christ" (v. 21, Gr. *phobos*) and "see that she respects (Gr. *phobētai*) her husband" in verse 33 are linked by the rhetorical device of *inclusio,* by which the opening and closing parts of a discussion match and form the terminal point of a section in classical Greek prose.

Second, even if the paraenetic call in verse 21 to mutual submission leads to a consideration of the role of women in worship, we still need to inquire whether the analogy of Christ-the-church is primary or secondary. Is the writer chiefly interested in the model of husband and wife together, drawing on Christ and the church as illustration? Or is the basic pattern a christological-ecclesiological one, which he uses to enforce teaching on the marital relationship? This issue is really a fundamental one, since how it is decided will determine the nature of the headship ascribed to both Christ (as head of the church) and man-as-husband (as head of his wife) in verse 23. Behind the issue is a hermeneutical question: What may we surmise was the occasion for the author to get into this question in the first place, and what are the options for locating a life setting of this section in the church scene of his time?

Both these concerns—of the primal model and of a suggested contingency in the life of the churches reflected in Ephesians—will need to be kept in mind in our bid adequately to exegete the text, though they are both problem-fraught matters.

It will, however, be helpful if we can set down in advance of our exegesis the four sets of correspondence between the Christ-church parallel and the man-woman relationship.

1. Christ is the head of the church, his body; and in the ordering of creation, according to the Pauline teaching of I Cor. 11:3, man occupies a place of headship over woman. This is elaborated in I Tim. 2:13 on grounds of the Genesis story and its chronological sequence but also based on woman's alleged inferiority in rabbinic anthropology.

68

2. Christ requires the obedience of his people, who are subject to him (v. 24). The inference is made that woman too is to be dependent upon man in all things. The last phrase widens the (disputed) Pauline teaching on the woman's role in public assembly (I Cor. 14:33*b*–34) and possibly the previous discussion in Eph. 5:19–21, extending it to all parts of the relationship and not simply to the arrangements of public worship.

3. Christ sets his love on the church and has redeemed it (vv. 25–27). The chief point already found in 5:1–2 is made in application at verse 28: let husbands love their wives like this.

4. Christ who looks on his church as part of himself, as his body, cares for it (vv. 29–30). In marriage the husband has a responsibility for his spouse.

The central, organizing phrase in this pericope (5:22–33) is found in verse 31 where Gen. 2:24 is quoted. The point made by this appeal to Genesis is the same as that in Mark 10:7–8. God created humankind as man and woman; they so yearn for each other that they are ready to leave their earthly parents. As Wolfgang Schrage (see Bibliography, under Gerstenberger) observes, marriage sets up so fundamental a relationship between man and woman that it relativizes and even terminates the original and universal relationship of the family unit in Israel's life. Not all Jewish texts have this deep thought, however. I Esdras 4:20–22 cites Gen. 2:24 as a sign of man's lust and willingness to be dominated by his wife.

Yet domination by either sex is not the way our author views the relationship. His primary appeal, as we saw, is to the example set by the heavenly Lord and his spouse, the church. This fact controls his understanding of the ambiguous term "subject," or perhaps better "be submissive" (vv. 21, 22, 24). As part of the domestic instructions found in other sections of the New Testament (Col. 3:18; I Peter 3:1–6; I Tim. 2:11–15) the call is sometimes taken to be one to blind obedience, docile servility, and unthinking subservience. It is then accepted that apostolic teaching was parallel with, say, Plutarch's marriage rules: "Women are to be praised if they subordinate themselves to their husbands" (*Praecepta Conjugalia* 33) or Philo's position in the same vein (Philo, *Hypothetica* 7:3). Yet it must be questioned whether this pattern of authority is what the New Testament codes are saying (with the possible exception of I Tim. 2:13–15 where some kind of feminine inferiority drawn from rabbinic arguments seems to be in mind).

69

There were other strands of marriage advice in the contemporary world. Plutarch qualifies his rather strict summons with the following: "The husband should rule over his wife not as a despot over a thing, but rather as the soul over the body, empathizing and permeated with affection" (*Praecepta Conjugalia* 33). Above all, the call to submission is modified by the phrase "in the Lord" (Col. 3:18), and it is part of the general summons to mutual consent in a spirit of yieldedness (Eph. 5:21), parallel at least in tone with I Peter 3:7. If we permit the word's etymology to add its weight, it is clear that submit/submissiveness cannot carry the sense of degrading servility, since I Cor. 15:28 shows how submission characterizes the relationship between Christ and the Father, and elements of voluntary consent and agreement are found in other places where the term is employed (I Cor. 14:32; 16:16) as well as Eph. 5:24.

The present paragraph is outstanding, however, for the addition it makes to a Christian perception of how men and women are related in society and in marriage. In a word, it is the christological model that predominates. The author proceeds from two fundamental premises: (1) There is a sacred nuptial union between Christ and his church, and (2) the outstanding characteristic of that holy marriage is a love that initiates and sustains the relationship, calling for an answering acceptance and consent. The operative and link term is "join" (v. 31) which the LXX uses of Israel's covenant with Yahweh (Deut. 10:20; II Kings 18:6).

Paul's teaching on marriage should first be studied in I Cor. 7:1-7. Celibacy is his preference, but it is a charism (gift-in-grace) not intended for all people. If one finds oneself faced with a choice, one should choose to remain unmarried (I Cor. 7:26-28)—a conclusion Paul draws on limited eschatological grounds, namely, that the end is near and one should not be burdened with extra anxieties by having to care for wife and children. Yet Paul's realism knows that human sex drives are strong, and it is only in marriage that a sexual partnership finds its adequate and legitimate fulfillment (I Cor. 7:3-5). He does respect the dignity and integrity of both the married and the unmarried state for both sexes (I Cor. 7:8, 25-38) but sees in the union of husband and wife a model for the church (II Cor. 11:2-3). Nothing more is said by him about the procreation of offspring or the maintenance of family life. When he has occasion to cite Gen. 2:24 (in I Cor. 6:16), its purpose is to emphasize the sacredness and exclusivity of the marital union as a protest against promiscuity and prostitution.

It is left to the writer of Ephesians to draw out the full import of this Pauline pastoralia. We may list the several ways he chooses to achieve an extension and enforcement of the master's teaching.

1. The sacred marriage motif goes back to Old Testament roots. Yahweh's choice of and marriage to Israel is a frequent theme in the prophets (Hos. 2:16; Isa. 54:4–5; 62:4–5; Ezek. 16:7–8). The rabbis took these passages and used them to eulogize the covenant between God and his people at Sinai in terms of a marriage contract (cf. Philo, *de Cherubim* 13). As Moses played the role of mediator, so Paul saw his task as one who led the bride to her groom (II Cor. 11:2; cf. John 3:29). Paul's authority appears less explicitly in Ephesians 5, but it does underlie verse 32 to buttress the claim that the sacred marriage may be read out of the Genesis text and so provide a paradigm of behavior for human partners. The "great mystery" is a typical idiom in this letter for God's saving plan, once concealed but now made known through Paul's Gentile mission and ministry. "I take it to mean" implies that Paul's mind is being appealed to in the debate that evidently centered on a gnosticizing disdain of marriage (as in I Tim. 4:3; Heb. 13:4). The Pauline advocate sides with his mentor to emphasize the goodness of creation (God made them male and female) and the binding character of marital fidelity (I Cor. 6:12–20). Yet he moves beyond him by citing Gen. 2:24 for its christological-ecclesiological interpretation, and he claims Paul's mind for it.

2. The primacy of love *(agapē)* is evident, seen in the line "Husbands, love your wives, as Christ loved the church" (v. 25). Love takes on one of its noblest forms when it is spelled out concretely in terms of self-surrender, sacrifice, and holy design. The author is building on I Corinthians 13 yet adding a soteriological dimension. He turns to such Pauline expressions as Gal. 2:20 as well as his earlier remark in 1:4 to drive home the point of a love that gives for the well-being of its beloved. The sacramental life of the church in baptism is in view as well (v. 26; Titus 3:5), drawn from I Cor. 6:11. This kind of loving defines and delimits the meaning of headship, both Christ's and the husband's.

The paraenetic appeal is registered in verse 28, with a jarring note detected in the words "love their wives as [they love]

71

their own bodies." Along with verses 29 and 33 this sentiment seems to smack of utilitarian ethics and a naive altruism. There must be a historical reason behind this appeal to loving one's *own body*. The answer, as we suggested, lies in a denigration of marriage among some Asian Christians who devalued all bodily existence as sinful and called for an ascetic way of life. The Pauline pastor will have none of this and so resorts to an exalting of marriage by the technique of using Paul's teaching on the church as like a body (I Cor. 12:12ff.; Rom. 12:4–5) and extending it in a realistic fashion. For him, the church *is* Christ's body (see 1:22–23; 3:6; 4:4) and Christians are members of it (4:16, 25) not only in the sense of I Cor. 6:19; 12:27 but in the deeper way that husband and wife became "one flesh," that is, no longer two persons but one (Eph. 2:14) and bonded together in a corporeal existence, nourished and sustained by this mutual relationship where each needs the other.

Verse 33 sums up. It looks back to verse 25 with the notes of love sounded, and even farther to verse 21 to form an *inclusio* with the call to respect/reverence. From the nexus of Christ-the-church the argument, polemically slanted, is made that husbands imitate Christ the lover and wives play the role of the church whose privilege (in this context) is to render submission. This line of reason may explain why he never tells wives to love their husbands, not because love is not appropriate as a human response to another's love, whether human or divine, but because in the primary model of the church joined to Christ, it is obedience and submission that the church offers to its Lord. The Christian's love *for* God is found in Paul only twice (Rom. 8:28; I Cor. 2:9 [in quotation]).

3. As marriage is lifted up as worthy and full of honor—since there is the highest precedent in the nuptial union of Christ and his bride—so family life is commended (6:1–4), and on similar grounds, namely, by an appeal to authoritative Scripture (Exod. 20:12; Deut. 5:16; 22:7). Fathers are singled out for special admonition, with encouragements to discipline and to instruct their children (both parts of education in ancient pedagogy) that add a positive note to Col. 3:21.

Ephesians 6:5–9
Relations of Masters and Slaves

This part of the station code (a name used for instructions that give advice as to the proper ordering of various members of a well-ordered household in Hellenistic society) treats of a real problem in early Christianity. The church was born into a social world in which human slavery was an accepted institution sanctioned by law and unquestioned even by high-minded moralists. The issue facing the believers was not one of acceptance of slavery per se or of how to react to a demand for its abolition (neither in I Cor. 7:20–24 nor in the note to Philemon does Paul hint at this). Rather, it was the way slaves were to accept their status and the way Christian slave owners were to treat the slaves in their control.

Modern readers of these verses (along with parallels in Col. 3:22–25 and other sections like I Peter 2:18–21; I Tim. 6:1–2; Titus 2:9–10) need to recall the historical circumstances of the first-century world and be on their guard lest they ask questions of New Testament writings that do not come within the purview of the authors. Slavery is a case in point. Otherwise we shall be amazed (and maybe scandalized) that the call here in Ephesians as elsewhere is one to obedience and not to revolt. The latter course would have been suicidal, given the power structures of Greco-Roman society.

Verse 5, with its summons to acquiescence and not open protest, is characteristic of New Testament teaching on slavery. Yet a note is sounded that goes some way toward ameliorating the slaves' lot and humanizing the system now judged to be barbaric. "Obey . . . as you would obey Christ" (NIV) resonates with a distinctive Christian reminder that allegiance to the Lord and a following of his pattern make life bearable as well as conduce to a positive witness to the world. Being "slaves of Christ," recalling I Cor. 7:22–23, will impart an unheard-of tone to work even if one is compelled to do it by the constraints of an unjust system. Service rendered with goodwill would sometimes bring its reward, as work is done with conscientiousness and integrity.

73

Present duties of slaves, though set within the bounds of the master-slave relationship, are lifted onto a new level in verse 8. The realized eschatology of this letter still makes room for future rewards. At the judgment seat (I Cor. 4:5; II Cor. 5:10; Rom. 14:12) human endeavors will be scrutinized and tested; this prospect awaits all professed believers, irrespective of social status and station.

So the discussion moves on to consider the slave owners. They too are bidden to act in a manner that befits their calling as church members. There is a caution registered against an overbearing disposition and a reminder that, though they are "masters" (Gr. *kyrioi*) of their slaves, they too have a heavenly Master *(kyrios)*. That Master cannot be bribed or corrupted to act in a way that would suggest favoritism or giving special regard to the influential.

In Col. 3:25 the same idea of impartiality is found, but with a different slant. There the call to slaves is not to exploit their Christian masters—perhaps with an eye on Onesimus, who (presumably) took money from Philemon and ran off. The local situation at Colossae is not reflected in Ephesians which transposes the teaching into a more general ethical rubric.

Ephesians 6:10–20
The Christian Warfare and the Apostle's Request

In this final section of the document the church's vocation in the hostile world is much in evidence. The reality of evil powers becomes the backdrop for the author's concern to admonish the readers and perhaps to temper the all-too-optimistic tone which belongs to the idea of the church as already raised with Christ and elevated in the heavenly realm (1:22–23; 2:6; 3:10). So the call to steadfastness under trial is sounded as the congregations are summoned to prepare for conflict—a common theme indeed in paraenetic parts of New Testament letters in general. See, for instance, Rom. 16:20; I Cor. 16:13; I Peter 5:8–9; James 5:8; and II Peter 3:17. Two interesting points emerge from this comparison. One is that there is no counterpart in Colossians to the admonition commencing at 6:10; second, Ephesians is unique in that it considerably extends the picture of the conflict to embrace supraterrestrial opponents of the church. The earlier references to Satan as the church's enemy (I Cor. 5:5; II Cor. 11:14; Rom. 16:20) or the opponent of the Pauline mission (I Thess. 2:18; II Cor. 12:7) are expanded to lift the engagement to the upper regions where, in traditional Jewish apocalyptic, Satan had his abode. The nearest parallel is Rev. 12:7: "And there was war in heaven" (NIV).

Behind the human aspects of opposition and seduction (already hinted at in 2:2; 4:14; 5:6, but these are no more than allusions, quite general) the writer detects the presence of superhuman forces arrayed against the church. The assaults of demonic powers require heavenly aid to repel, and it is the epistle's conviction, in true Pauline fashion, that God has placed at the Christians' disposal all that is needed to resist such an attack. In particular, the various pieces of armor are listed.

The most recent study of the passage, by Clinton E. Arnold, correctly notes the heavy emphasis on power words in verses 10, 11, 13, 16; most of the terms are rare in the New Testament, but they recall 1:10. The categorizing of demonic agents in verse 12 as principalities, powers, cosmocrats is again exceptional. And it is a good suggestion that the author is led into this exhortatory appeal because he sees the audience threatened by a fear of the demonic and exposed to a tendency to defect under pressure. Hence the call: "Resist" as well as "Watch," "Pray," "Be alert."

As to the genre of the passage, most modern scholars note the parallels with the battle motif drawn from Isa. 11:4–5; 52:7; 59:17, with lesser probability from Wisd. Sol. 5:17–20 and 1QM (the War Scroll) from Qumran. The descriptive writing is full of Old Testament echoes, such as the "girding" of oneself by tucking in the folds of a garment to form a belt—a sign of readiness (6:14; cf. Job 38:3; 40:7; Nah. 2:1; Luke 12:37; 17:8; Acts 12:8). But the nearest source of the author's writing, strangely overlooked in some discussions, is the model of the Roman soldier ready for battle. Perhaps this was suggested to the writer by the tradition (found in Col. 4:18) that the historical Paul wore chains in captivity and was placed under guard (v. 20). As the Christian apostle, he looked to his friends in the Asian churches, where he found support to stand by him in *his* conflict (Col. 2:1); now

75

his cause is entrusted to his disciples who shared his devotion, his readiness to be faithful, and to engage boldly in the same kind of conflict he endured when put under duress by his Roman captors. The points of comparison with the soldier on duty may be noted.

The text spells out the responsibility the soldier has. He must equip himself adequately for the fray. Yet as the armor is God's (v. 11), meaning presumably "the armor God himself wears" in his engagement with opposing powers (so Isa. 59:17; Wisd. Sol. 5:17–20), no provision is lacking. No part of the body is unprotected. Like Achilles whose armor was fashioned by the gods (*Iliad* 18.478–616), the believer's protection as he faces the enemy is complete and sure. Hence the reminder: "the entire armor," offered as a defense in the evil day of eschatological struggle (5:16).

The items listed are taken from the model of the soldier at the place of duty and ready for battle. The belt is a sign of this preparedness, as the Romans spoke of *miles accinctus,* meaning a soldier on parade, with his belt (Lat. *cingulum*) fastened in position (Tacitus, *Annals* 11.18).

Breastplate (cf. Isa. 59:17; Wisd. Sol. 5:18) is a picture taken from the prophetic literature, meaning a crusade against social evil and a call for redress. Feet need shoes for marching and for mission (Isa. 52:17), as Paul had taught (Rom. 10:15). To cover all of his body, there was the "shield of faith" (the Greek *thyreos* represents the Latin *scutum,* specially effective against the enemy's flaming missiles). This Roman shield was large and quadrangular, designed to catch the barrage of ignited arrows hurled at it.

Two further pieces of equipment make up the balance of the soldier's dress. The helmet of salvation (from Isa. 59:17; contrast Wisd. Sol. 5:18, where God is said to wear the helmet of doom) marks Yahweh's mission to vindicate his people and to promote his cause in the earth. The sword is wielded with cutting power when "the word of God" is uttered (Isa. 11:4 comes in a passage also couched in military idiom).

Although there is no counterpart in a soldier's equipment, the continued list of "prayer and supplication" is evidently intended to be included in the category. The link idea which suggests this continuation of items in the armory is the Spirit who inspires prayer (v. 18), as Paul taught (Rom. 8:28ff.; Phil. 4:6; I Thess. 5:17–19). "Supplication," that is, a prayer for others,

76

is related to "all the saints," those who form God's people, both Jews and Gentiles, of the new covenant (1:1, 18; 3:6–8). This prayerful regard is needed at all times, but more so at every critical juncture (5:16) when alertness and perseverance are requisite qualities.

From general admonition to encourage prayer for Paul's work and legacy in Asia the thought moves on in verse 19 to a personalized reference. At first glance this looks to be similar to the appeal in II Cor. 1:11. There is a difference, however. Where previous requests for the apostle's life have been set in a personal framework (his safety, his relations with the churches), now the plea is directly connected with the apostolic ministry committed to Paul as apostle to the Gentiles and hence to those who came after him. So where verses 19 and 20 look to be a highly individualized utterance of the historical Paul, on examination the life situation behind this exceptional appeal reflects more probably a corporate need. Paul's followers are voicing their concern in his name for the mission in Asian congregations. They use the tradition in Col. 4:2–4 as a basis to express the need for the churches' prayers that the same apostolic work, begun by Paul and continued by his disciples, may not be retarded by timidity or wither through an indifference to or neglect of the truths represented uniquely by Paul in his lifetime. At stake is "the mystery of the gospel"—a term already explained and illustrated as the uniting of both Jews and Gentiles in one body (3:4–6; 5:32); it must be defended with a courage akin to that shown by Paul in his (final) imprisonment. He took for himself the title of Christ's "ambassador" (II Cor. 5:20, though this may be a term derived from tradition Paul takes over to modify in 5:20*b*). But unlike court personnel, he enjoyed no diplomatic immunity. Quite the contrary; he exchanged his days of freedom for confinement "in chains" (whether in Ephesus, Col. 4:18, or at Rome, according to Acts 26:29).

Personal Report and Final Greetings

EPHESIANS 6:21–24

This closing section parallels so closely Col. 4:7–8 that we may suspect a borrowing on the part of the author of Ephesians. One small piece of evidence tips the scales in the direction of this side of the borrowing and incidentally is a pointer to the conclusion that Ephesians represents a community product. At Col. 4:8 the phrase "that you may know *how we are*" (Gr. *ta peri hēmōn*) refers naturally to Paul and his colleague Timothy (Col. 1:1). But no such dual sender is found in Eph. 1:1, and Paul's solo name and authority recur throughout (1:15; 3:1, 14; 4:1; 5:20, 21). Yet the plural form "how we are" is retained in the text of 6:22 even though only Paul as an individual is apparently the writer and sender. Here is a clear—if minor—sign that Ephesians is indebted to Colossians and that a group of Paulinists is at work in this final postscript.

Tychicus was the informant to the Asian churches of the circumstances of Paul's captivity. The break between verses 20 and 21 in the RSV is there to mark a change of subject, and the lifting of data from Col. 4:7–8 is intended to add a touch of verisimilitude and sound the note of authority on Paul's behalf. It may also be brought in to illustrate the kind of care the apostle exhibited for his congregations in the Gentile world. The tradition in Colossians is appealed to as a reinforcement of what has run through the entire letter, namely, a defense and restatement of the Pauline gospel in the face of a threat posed to the Asian churches now that Paul is no longer on hand. What better support for this appeal could there be than an exact citation of Paul's solicitude for a church in the area? Tychicus is a prime candidate to offer this endorsement, since he, like his master, is known as a "faithful minister" (v. 21; cf. 3:7 for same term, *diakonos*) as well as a "dear brother."

78

The closing greeting is slightly longer than in the Pauline corpus, for example, Phil. 4:23, and is couched in more general terms by the use of impersonal appellation ("the brothers and sisters") rather than the more direct "you." Addressees are (uniquely) blessed with the designation "all who love our Lord Jesus Christ" (borrowed in essence from I Cor. 16:22) with "an undying love" (NRSV; NIV is similar). The Greek has simply *en aphtharsia,* with no word corresponding to "love." *Aphtharsia,* immortality, is not frequent in Paul and may be part of the benediction, "Grace and immortality" (so NEB). Dibelius-Greeven offer a striking translation by giving a spatial sense to the noun, grace . . . from our Lord Jesus Christ who (lives) in imperishable (glory). Cf. I Tim. 1:17; James 2:1. To support this unusual wording we may appeal to the appropriateness of a solemn close to a letter that began "in the heavenly places" (1:3), continued with a tribute to the church's exaltation (2:6), and now fittingly closes by pointing to the enthroned Lord in the heavenly realm.

THE BOOK OF
Colossians

Introduction

Introducing Colossians

Of all the letters written by the apostle Paul the one addressed to the church at Colossae poses the problem of our limited knowledge of its setting. We would like to know far more than we do about the issues that made Paul write in response to the needs of his readers. We can only offer some suggestions as to those matters, both theological and practical, which occasioned his letter.

But the contribution of Colossians to our understanding of Paul's mind and pastoral ministry is considerable. It is this factor which makes the letter so fascinating and worth our attention today. It shows the person of Jesus Christ as the answer to human questions about the cosmos of which we are such an insignificant, yet unique, part. Insignificant we may be, and terrified by the vast reaches of outer space, yet our life has meaning. For our human existence was once owned and dignified by the coming of God into our world in his Son. Henceforth the character of God is spelled out in terms of that human life. And the pattern of human existence is set and shaped by him as "the new humanity" in whose image a distinctive quality of life is born and is growing. These central concerns of Paul's letter give it a relevance for us as Christian leaders and readers.

When Paul wrote to the Christians living at Colossae, a town in what is now modern Turkey, the city's population consisted mainly of indigenous Phrygian and Greek settlers. But Josephus *(Antiquities* 12.149) records that Antiochus III in the early part of the second century B.C.E. had brought several thousand Jews from Mesopotamia and Babylon and settled them in Lydia and Phrygia. Colossae, in Paul's day, was thus a cosmopolitan city in which diverse cultural and religious elements met and mingled. This is quite possibly a serious factor in the total situation that provoked the Colossian crisis, which followed the emergence of a religious and theosophical teaching that threatened to engulf the church there. As we shall observe, the nature of this teaching was composite and was made up partly of Jewish elements and partly of ideas belonging to the world of Hellenistic religious philosophy and mysticism. Colossae was a cultural center where this potpourri might well have been expected. Thus it is not surprising that it was the Colossian congregation in a city partly Jewish-Oriental but chiefly Greek-Phrygian that became the target of an assault in the name of a syncretistic religion. To judge from 1:21, 27; 2:13, however, the composition of the Colossian church was predominantly Gentile-Christian, leading one commentator to conclude that as a background to the letter even the Judaism in the towns of the Lycus valley has to be viewed in the setting of Hellenistic culture. Three chief ingredients of the latter were Phrygian nature worship, Iranian astrological speculation, and wisdom teaching drawn from the mystery cults (Lähnemann, p. 104).

The Threat to Faith and the Colossian Crisis

Perhaps quite unconsciously the church at Colossae was being exposed to a false teaching that Paul regarded as both subversive of the faith and inimical to it. Part of the occasion of his letter may be traced to the presence of this threatened danger and the need to rebut the error that lay at the heart of the aberration. The letter to the Colossians is thus "concerned with those aspects of the gospel which were chiefly threatened by the Colossian heresy—the uniqueness of the person of Christ, in whom the plenitude of deity was embodied; the perfection of the redeeming and reconciling work accomplished by his death on the cross, and the spiritual liberty enjoyed by all who by faith were united to him" (Bruce, *Commentary,* pp. 26–27). But, as Henry Chadwick has shown (1:270–275), Paul's defense of the apostolic faith goes hand in hand with an apologetic statement of that faith to the intellectual world of his day. In this sense his letter to the Colossians is one of the earliest Christian "apologies," or defensive statements of the faith over against its rivals and competitors, that we possess.

What was the exact nature of the error that Paul denounces and combats? Nowhere in the letter does Paul give a formal definition of it, and its chief lineaments can be detected only by piecing together and interpreting his positive counterarguments. There are, however, some crucial and combative passages in which he seems to be actually quoting the slogans and watchwords of the teachers, and these form invaluable clues in our attempt at literary detection. The hope is that these citations will enable us to build up a sort of identi-kit picture of the teaching against which Paul sets his face. The verses (in NRSV) in question are:

1:19 "For in him all the fullness of God was pleased to dwell"
2:18 "insisting on self-abasement and worship of angels"
2:21 "Do not handle, Do not taste, Do not touch" (the clearest instance)
2:23 "promoting self-imposed piety, humility, and severe treatment of the body"

And, quite possibly, the allusions to "elemental spirits of the universe" (2:8, 20) pick up terms that were being advocated as an important part of the cult.

Even from this short list we are able to see that the threat to apostolic faith and life was both theoretical and practical. Part of the teaching was related to a theological matter and centered on the question, Where is God's true presence to be found and how may human beings gain access to that presence? The answer evidently (for we must bring in the data from the late-second-century Gnostic systems to aid us) came back from these Colossian teachers: God's fullness is distributed throughout a series of emanations from the divine, stretching from heaven to earth. These "eons" or offshoots of deity must be venerated and homage paid to them as "elemental spirits" or angels or gods inhabiting the stars. They rule destiny, control human life, and hold the entrance into the divine realm in their keeping. Christ is one of them, but only one among many.

The other question was intensely practical. How may one prepare for a vision of heavenly realities as part of a rite of passage into the divine presence? The reply was given in terms of a rigorous discipline of asceticism and self-denial. Abstinence, especially from food and drink; observance of holy seasons for fasting and affliction of the soul (2:16); possibly a life of celibacy

83

and mortification of the human body (2:21, 23)—all these exercises and taboos were prescribed as part of the regimen to be accepted if the Christians at Colossae were ever to gain "fullness of life" (2:10).

In brief compass, this is the sketch or "cartoon" boldly brushed onto the canvas in deft strokes by these verses. Can we now add more color and distinctiveness to the picture of this doctrine and way of life? But before we get down to fill in something of the cultural and intellectual background, we should pause to inquire why Paul was so vehemently opposed to this system of thought and practice. Three reasons are offered.

Paul quickly discerned that such a wrongheaded cosmology *meant a derogatory attitude toward Jesus Christ.* If Paul's teaching on the person and place of Jesus Christ has any meaning at all, it is emphatic on the point that Christ is unique and without peer. Both his relationship to God and his role as revealer and redeemer are stamped with a finality and completeness that cannot be compromised. To Paul, any suggestion that Christ was one mediator in a series of intermediaries between heaven and earth would be effectively to rob Christ of his dignity and to paralyze Christian salvation at a vital nerve center. Nor could Paul tolerate any thought that Jesus Christ had only partially revealed God or imperfectly secured the church's redemption. This would open the door to the need for various supplemental contributions to human reconciliation and so introduce the element of uncertainty into the Christian's fellowship with God. If Christ's reconciling work were incomplete, what assurance is there that one has placated the right angel spirit or sufficiently understood the apparatus needed to gain a full salvation—on the principle that Christ's achievement is not sufficient by itself?

This setting explains much of the insistence that Paul gives to the cosmic and reconciling role of the church's Lord, especially in the impressive diptych of 1:15–20. Here the two sides of Christ's office are fully described. He is both cosmic agent in creation (1:15–17) and the church's reconciler through whom God restores harmony between God and creation (1:18–20). No loophole is left for any intruding eon to come between God and Christ, on the one hand, or between Christ and the world and the church on the other. In him (not in any spirit or angel or

84

other intelligence) the totality of the divine fullness dwells, at the pleasure of God (1:19) and for the security of the church, which is assured thereby of fullness of life in him (2:9-10).

The comprehensiveness of Christ's reconciling work is such as to include even those alien powers which the Hellenistic world thought of as hostile to humanity. The risen Lord is both their creator and their ruler. He engineered their coming into being (1:16) in the beginning; and by his victory over death he has taken his place as "the head" or ruler over all cosmic forces, angelic and demonic (2:10). In the new beginning, which is marked by his resurrection, he takes his rank as the preeminent one (1:18), having gained the victory over all the evil powers that first-century society most feared (2:15).

In a strange way the syncretistic teachers not only cast a role for Jesus Christ that demoted him from his pinnacle as God's image and son; they seem to have doubted the reality of his humanity also. Yet this was part of their general understanding of God and the world. In their view, God was remote and inaccessible except through a long chain of intermediaries. Jesus Christ was one of these, but he was sufficiently related to God to share the divine abhorrence for any *direct* contact with matter. To the Gnostic mind, God was pure spirit, and the world stood over against God as something alien and despicable. On this assumption, no incarnation—a veritable coming of the divine into human life—was thinkable, and the net result was the rise of docetism. This term (from the Greek verb "to seem," "to appear") says that Jesus Christ came from the divine side of reality but only dressed himself in human nature as a token appearance. It was a piece of playacting when God wore a mask of humanity on the stage of human history, giving the appearance of being human but really being still God-in-disguise.

Is there evidence of this teaching of a divine charade at Colossae? We cannot say so definitely, but Paul has some verses that seem directly to oppose what looks like this type of teaching. At the head of the list are those texts which anchor Christ's incarnation in an acceptance of our "flesh," that is, our human nature, weak, frail, and exposed to temptation (1:22; 2:11). His death on the cross is vividly pictured by the reference to his blood (1:20), and his afflictions are mentioned (1:24).

Christ's work of reconciliation was accomplished at great cost, we read. It was not by some wave of the hand that God

85

took action to forgive our sins (1:14) and trespasses (2:13). It required God's coming to our deepest levels of human experience—Christ's taking a human body (2:9) and being subject to demonic powers that sought to overcome him and hold him prey (2:15). They succeeded insofar as to put him on a cross (2:14), where his blood was spilt (1:20) and he died a real death (1:22). Moreover, his sufferings were real, and those who continue the work he came to achieve—Paul himself is his representative in this enterprise (1:24)—must expect also to tread a path of tribulation. So the apostle is a prisoner (4:18) as "apostle of Christ Jesus by the will of God" (1:1), not in spite of being such.

Possessing Christ as the repository of "all the treasures of wisdom and knowledge" (2:3) is the sufficient antidote to this teaching which casts a slur on the church's Lord and God's very essence (2:2). Moreover, losing one's grip on him as the head (of God? I Cor. 11:3; of the church? 1:18) is to forfeit one's only hope (2:19). But what lies at the basis of this uncompromising statement? Is Paul simply opposing the Colossian errorists in his own name and arrogantly anathematizing all who do not choose to agree with him? Clearly not in view of the contrast he draws between "human tradition" (2:8, 22) and the deposit of an apostolic teaching concerning Christ which he adheres to and has passed on to the Colossian church through Epaphras. It is the contrast between human "philosophy" and divine "revelation" committed to the apostles.

The key verses here are 2:6–7. Paul is reflecting on the past experience of the readers' Christian standing. From Epaphras they had learned of God's grace (1:7), and he in turn came to their city as Paul's proxy and missioner. What he taught was the "gospel," and this was certified as "the word of the truth" (1:5), that is, it carried the ring of truth as a God-given message. The Colossians had accepted it as such and had been drawn to "faith in Christ Jesus" (1:4).

Paul can therefore express his deep gratitude to God for this ready reception and cordial acceptance of the saving word. Now (in 2:6) he recalls this in the statement that the Christ they had received as Lord was the Christ of apostolic proclamation. It was no human tradition they had assented to; rather, they had been "taught" the true word and had begun to build their lives on Christ, to take root in the soil of divine truth and to bear fruit in Christian living (1:6). They had come to know God's grace *as it really is* (1:6) and not in reliance on any human tradition.

86

There is a subtle play on words here, which is difficult to see in the English versions. It is the contrast that Paul has in view between acceptance of "human tradition" (Gr. *paradosis,* 2:8) and "teachings" (Gr. *didaskalia,* 2:22) and the obedience to apostolic tradition, represented in 2:6: "as you received" (Gr. *parelabete:* the complementary verb is "what was handed on to you," *paradidonai,* as in I Cor. 11:23; 15:3; Gal. 1:9–14) and 2:7: "as you were taught" (Gr. *edidachthēte*). It is the stark contrast between a man-made religion, both cleverly contrived and laying claim to a kind of wisdom ("philo-sophy") but ersatz and ineffectual (2:23) and the true word which is entrusted to the apostolic preachers and which centers in Christ, the mystery and revelation of God (2:2; 4:3).

A second reason for Paul's vehement opposition to the Colossian teachers was that his theology was always closely connected with the need to live the Christian life in this world. Theology, for him, was not an intellectual game making its appeal to the curious-minded or offering a pastime to fill the vacant hour. Theology was a matter of life and death. What God is and has done in Christ and is doing by his Spirit in the church and the world are all matters of vital concern because they impinge directly upon our understanding of life and human destiny. Paul can intertwine profound theological interest and pressing ethical claims in an amazing way, as he does memorably in Phil. 2:1–12. At Colossae, the dangerous speculation about God, angels, and access to the divine takes on a fearsome aspect because *it robs the church of its Christian liberty.*

The connecting "therefore" in 2:16 is a good illustration. Precisely because Christ has overcome the church's enemies in the heavenly world by divesting these spiritual forces of their power to tyrannize over human life, the Colossians are bidden to accept their freedom from the bondage of bad religion.

The Colossian teachers made much of dietary taboos and ascetic practices. Paul sees these as a threat to the charter of freedom in Christ, already secured in him by his death and risen life. The call he sounds is one to a new quality of Christian living, unencumbered by false inhibitions and man-made regulations (2:22; cf. Gal. 5:1). These prescriptions and rules belong to the shadows (2:7). He asks, Why remain in the dismal half-light of fear and uncertainty when the sun is high in the sky, filling the world with light? Seek a life that draws on Christ's own risen power (3:1–3), as those who share an inheritance in light (1:12) with all God's people, since you have died with him to those agents of demonic powers which tried to get rid of him on the cross (2:20). Have no truck with their authority, since it has been broken once for all, and don't compromise or forfeit your Christian liberty (2:8) by surrendering to a specious philosophy that is deceptive and to a type of religion that can only be branded as man-made and therefore fake (2:23; see commentary on this verse).

Paul clearly does not mince his words or hold back in his forthright judgment. The reason can only be that what is at stake is something vital and precious. For this apostle, nothing would be more central to the Christian life than his and his people's freedom in Christ in which what counts is not observance of human tradition (2:8, 22) or man-devised rules (2:20) or a way of life that ignores the tremendous difference that Christ has made (2:17). For him, the essence of "religion" is Christ, and the mainspring of morality is a death-and-resurrection experience (signified in a believing response in baptism) in which the old nature dies to self and sin and the new nature is received as a gift from God (2:11–13; 3:9–12). It is that new humanity which is Christ-living-in-his-body, the church, which provides both the sphere in which Christian morality is defined and the motive power by which Christians are able to live together in the one family of God. This has been called the *koinōnia* motive, by which is meant that Paul's ethical norms are found by following the call, "Act as members of Christ's body." His counsels in chapter 3 of our epistle include a teaching on the true self-discipline as well as a much fuller statement of how Christian men and women relate to one another in their church fellowship and in contemporary society. They are called into the "one body" (3:15) with love giving coherence to all the ethical qualities that characterize that new life-style (3:11-12).

The contrast is seen at its clearest by setting two verses side by side. In 2:20 Paul asks in amazement how the Colossian believers have so readily given hospitality to false teaching and so yielded their freedom: "Why do you submit to regulations?" These are the rules which impose false demands, false because they have been met in Christ's cross (2:14). At the opposite end of the spectrum to this restrictive code is the vocation of the Christian person whose entire life, in word and deed, is one of dedication to the Lord Jesus who came to give life in its fullness (2:10). It is small wonder, then, that the believer will show gratitude to God for such an expansive attitude toward life, world-affirming and full of *joie de vivre* (3:17; cf. 3:23).

A third reason Paul writes so incisively against the false doctrine, decrying its value (2:4) and labeling it no better than "empty deceit" (2:8), is seen in what he says about the spirit of those who are its self-appointed teachers. The promoter of this cult is a person who is "puffed up without cause by a human way of thinking" (2:18, NRSV). Literally translated, the last phrase would run: "by the mind of his flesh." This is the hallmark of the unregenerate individual (Rom. 8:7), and Paul is quick to identify the false prophet as a teacher who has no place in the church. J. B. Lightfoot thought that Paul is making use of a claim put forward by this one who insisted that he was directed by his "mind," that is, he was excogitating his novel teaching by drawing an inference about divine truth from his visionary experience. Paul caustically remarks that, if his mind is at work in this fantasy, it is a mind still held captive to his "flesh" (Gr. *sarx*), his own conceits and pride. "Flesh" here carries "the sense of natural man in his selfishness" (Percy, p. 79). It is pride which lay at the root of this claim to esoteric knowledge (cf. II Cor. 10:5). And for that reason Paul opposes this current teaching *because it ministers to human boasting and a haughty, exclusivist spirit.*

We should find a similar judgment in 2:23 (see commentary) where the regime of ascetic restrictions is misdirected and serves only to increase the devotee's sense of false security. It offers no remedy to keep one humble and dependent on God's grace; on the contrary, it inflates one's pride in self-achievement and gives a wrongful sense of self-congratulation that one is numbered among the fortunate who are better than the average run of Christians.

Paul's way of self-mastery is held out to all men and women, not restricted to a favored few. This epistle constantly returns to the theme of the universality of the gospel in the Pauline mission churches, and there is no mistaking the way this accent sounds a counterblast to heretical exclusiveness (see 1:6, 23, 28; 3:11).

Again, we may point to a contrast. What passes as a species of "humility" (2:18, 23) is little better than a mock piety, because the motive is wrong. What motivates these advocates at Colossae is a desire to make a proud claim and to belong to a select group of elite. The church members are warned to see the danger in this pretended religion's aspiration, to turn away from it, and to seek the true "humility" (3:12, same Greek word) as God's elect, who are no esoteric group in a self-contained circle but are coextensive with all Christian people throughout the world (1:23).

On every count, therefore, Paul has a low opinion of the novelties that lurk at the threshold of the Colossian congregation. He sees in their appearance a threat to faith and a dangerous deceit. He can entertain no serious discussion with such a way-out religion and such an offering of theosophical mishmash. The more eccentric and out of the way this cult seems to be, the greater danger he senses. For this first-century scientism is being advocated with enticing words (2:4) and in the name of what claims to be serious-minded and highly "intellectual" (2:8). The apostle calls it an empty delusion. This designation has suggested to Werner Bieder (pp. 62–66) how we should understand 2:4. A deliberate design on the part of the Colossian innovators is to be read into these words. They purposed to trick the Christians inside the church as part of a manipulative process of clever rhetoric and "the art of persuasion" (so Bieder translates the text in v. 4). In fine, they made false promises, offering a call to wisdom (2:23) that turns out to be, in Paul's estimation, nothing more than specious make-believe.

Yet name-calling is not enough. Paul will consider its nature and claim. He will expose its shallowness and peril. And he will fortify his Colossian friends to take their stand against this spurious religion.

It is time to examine its nature more closely.

The Colossian "Philosophy"

Two terms are used to fasten an identity label on the false teaching introduced at Colossae. They are "philosophy" (2:8) and "forced piety" (2:23, NEB). The latter term is not easily translatable (Gr. *ethelothrēskia*). Of the various possibilities, we prefer the rendering "fake religion."

What are the elements that went to make up this teaching?

Much was made of *astrology,* which centered on the importance accorded to "elemental spirits of the universe" (2:8, 20). This is a controverted phrase. The Greek phrase runs *ta stoicheia tou kosmou,* and the key word is *stoicheia.*

90

The basic meaning of *stoicheia* is "objects that stand in a row or that form a series." The most natural example of these objects is letters of the alphabet, which stand together in a line to make continuous writing. From this idea it is an easy step to reach the notion of "elements of learning," or, as we say, ABCs, meaning rudiments or basic principles. This is the sense of Heb. 5:12: "the elementary truths of God."

The translation "elements" came also to be applied to physical substances, as again in our modern speech when we talk of the "elements" as everything that goes to make up the natural world or the weather conditions! A New Testament reference to the physical components of the universe is II Peter 3:10, 12; and the ancients spoke of four such elements—earth, fire, water, air (see Schweizer, who thinks this is the best explanation of *stoicheia*).

In later Greek religious and philosophical thought the parts of the universe were put under the control of spirit-powers, and there was a tendency to divinize, if not the parts of earth, then the heavenly bodies. Diogenes Laertius speaks of "the twelve *stoicheia*" in regard to the signs of the zodiac, and the constellation of heavenly bodies is placed under the description of "immortal *stoicheion.*"

The final stage of this development is reached when the stars themselves are dignified with being not only dwelling places of the gods but divine in their own right, and so requiring to be venerated. This startling transition came about mainly because of the advent of Oriental astrology and occultism which, with its accompanying astral religion and dominant fatalism, haunted like a nightmare the soul of first-century people. The vacuum (caused by disillusion over the collapse of the Homeric gods who were like magnified men and women on Mount Olympus) was quickly filled with an all-embracing capitulation to "chance." People who came under the spell of star worship were made to feel that all things were ruled by "fate." The particular conjunction of the stars or planets under which people were born was of decisive importance and settled irretrievably their destiny. Hence the central place of the heavenly bodies in popular Hellenistic religion was established once the astrologers had capitalized on this yearning for a "religion" to fill the void.

91

What hope was there for a person in this setting of religious determinism and inevitability? One way of salvation was offered in a placating of the star deities, and by ascetic practices a possibility was held out for a person to escape from the mesh of inevitability and the hopeless round of uncertainty. Also, some deities were hailed as protectors of men and women on earth, and fellowship with these gods and goddesses raised the devotees above the circle of fate and iron-clad determinism. In that way the *stoicheia* could be overcome and their victims set free.

In this context and given the total situation of the Colossian teaching, opposed by Paul, which meaning of *stoicheia* seems most likely? Two alternatives form the main possibilities.

On the one hand, Paul is regarding the false system as "elementary teaching" either by Jewish or pagan ritualists in the sense that it is materialist at heart and exclusively tied to this world and therefore infantile. By contrast, Paul's gospel invites men and women to accept the freedom of Christ and to remain no longer in a kindergarten stage of religious taboos and restrictions (so Moule). Alternatively, Paul is branding this cult as false because it placed men and women under the control of powerful spirit intelligences that held them prey and that needed to be placated. Many reasons support the second interpretation.

1. The tenor of other polemical parts of the letter indicates Paul's belief in Christ's victory over demonic agencies (2:15; esp. 2:20).

2. Only this view explains Paul's repeated insistence that the divine "fullness" dwells in Christ, not in these cosmic forces (1:19; 2:9). They, on the contrary, owe their existence to him (1:15–20; 2:10).

3. The references in 2:16–17 to calendrical observances link up with the Jewish notion of angels who mediated the law (Acts 7:38, 53; Gal. 3:19; 4:9–10). Further, the relapse of the Galatian Christians to "the weak and beggarly elements" (Gr. *stoicheia*) may mean a return to the gods of paganism from which they had been converted (4:8–10). Paul can hardly imply that they were relapsing to simplistic forms of religion and that the effect of a superstitious evil eye of bewitchment (3:1) was calculated to answer their yearning for an uncomplicated faith.

4. Percy (p. 167) has argued cogently that Paul sets the *stoicheia* in direct antithesis to Christ (2:8) and this suggests that "for him the contrast lies not between spirit and matter . . . but between this age ruled by spirit-forces and Christ. It is the contrast between Greek and early Christian understandings of existence."

92

5. The practice of asceticism was encouraged by these teachers (2:20–23) as part of their discipline. It is likely that such was a preparatory exercise calculated to overcome hostile spirit powers and to induce a trancelike visionary experience (2:18).

6. "Worship of angels" (2:18) must be related to some kind of cultus, and the homage paid to these heavenly orders suggests that it is part of the same "philosophy" or theosophical system that venerated the star deities.

Our conclusion is that Paul's evidence suggests that the Colossian teaching was concerned to give a prominent place to angelic orders as custodians of human destiny. In current Hellenistic thought this was closely related to the stars and their patron deities. But Paul will have none of this in his insistence that all cosmic powers are dependent upon the preexisting Christ who entirely fills the universe and leaves no room for competing agencies, now that they are defeated and subservient to him. He alone gives meaning to the universe which coheres in him (1:16–17); and so he alone gives meaning and purpose to life (2:10).

Yet another tenet was championed by the innovators at Colossae. They evidently held a *dualism* that separated the high God from creation and taught that to attain to God a person must be delivered from the evil influence of material things. This "liberation" in later Gnostic religion was achieved along two quite diverse routes, one starting from the premise of matter, especially the human body, as evil, and the other treating matter as indifferent.

One path to Gnostic salvation was (as we have indicated) asceticism, which summoned the devotee to a life of abstinence and self-punishment. Paul preserves the actual wording of the slogans that were being advocated at Colossae (2:21, 23) and retorts that such denials—"Do not handle" (or possibly, "Do not engage in sex relations even within marriage"); "Do not taste" wine; "Do not touch" food (cf. I Tim. 4:1–4)—are of no value to counter "the indulgence of the flesh." That is, when these ascetic practices are used simply to prepare an initiate to enter a trancelike state and thereby to gain a vision of heavenly things (2:18), they serve only to inflate with pride and fill with vain knowledge and so bolster a person's "flesh," that is, one's unrenewed ego, which is puffed up by this experience. 93

Coupled with these ascetic practices was a code probably influenced by a type of Jewish religiosity with its observances of the Sabbath, feast days, and new moon celebrations (2:16); possibly the practice of circumcision (2:11); and Jewish dietary laws (2:21). Various suggestions have been made to pinpoint the cultural milieu of these practices. Lightfoot drew a comparison between these restrictions and the taboos and practices of the Essenes; and recently the Qumran texts from the Dead Sea area have shown that similar calendrical details were highly regarded among the Essene monks in that community. Yet it is doubtful that Essenism had penetrated to the Lycus valley, and there is a singular absence of debate over the Mosaic law and nomistic religion in the Colossian controversy.

F. O. Francis (see Bibliography) argues that Paul's opponents appealed to Exodus 19, which is used in Hebrews 12 as a foil to advance the idea of worshiping in heaven with the angels (Heb. 12:22, 28). Colossians 2:17 presents a contrast between shadow and substance, which also plays a decisive role in Hebrews. But Francis's view that the Colossian errorists stressed a sharing in heavenly worship *led by angels* is contradicted by 2:23, where the angelic worship is part of a rite performed by the devotees themselves.

Note on the Background of the False Teaching

The type of Judaism reflected in these chapters is a matter for continuing discussion. Clearly it is not the orthodox Judaism of the Palestinian rabbis, nor is it indubitably a sectarian wing of Essenism or Qumranism. A body of Continental scholars prefers to speak of a "Jewish Gnosticism" which combined with Christian elements to form the substance of the Colossian heresy.

The measure of success in finding in a Jewish gnosis the key to the Colossian heresy will be judged by a threefold presentation in the epistle itself.

1. The importance Paul gives to religious "knowledge" (Gr. *gnōsis*) seems to indicate that he has to deal with a situation in which the acquirement of esoteric knowledge needed to be refuted, as the apostle does in his repeated teaching (1:9-10; 2:3; 3:10, 16) on God's gift of knowledge and wisdom. But these terms are filled with a new connotation, based on the Old Testament meaning of "to know God," meaning to obey God's will and to walk in God's way.

94

2. The cosmological role ascribed to Christ is a highlighted feature of chapters 1 and 2. In the academic commentaries the

different lines of interpretation possible in regard to 1:15–20 are considered and some argue (correctly, we think) that Paul is not adopting Gnostic terminology in his ascriptions to the cosmic Christ of such titles as "image of God," "fullness of God," and "firstborn," but stands in the tradition of the wisdom scholars in Hellenistic Judaism.

3. The principal argument in favor of a first-century "gnosticism" (however we choose to define the term) in existence at Colossae and refuted in our letter is found in the polemic against an angel cult and a dualistic system. This takes us to the heart of the Gnostic worldview (now confirmed by the recent discovery of a Gnostic-Christian library at Nag Hammadi). Again we are hindered in our effort to press back behind Paul's words to what must have given rise to them in the Colossian church. Clearly there was a practice of angelic worship (2:18), and Paul goes out of his way to accentuate the teaching on cosmic reconciliation, with no part of the universe unaffected (1:15–20) and no hostile power unsubdued (2:15). The angelic superbeings (he counters) are reduced to impotence and are led in triumph. Some transcendental engagement between Christ and an enemy is envisaged, and peace is proclaimed after the end of the war is declared (1:20).

What is the type of dualism implied here? Some interpreters insist that it is a moral tension, not an ontological gulf which sets Christ in opposition to his rivals. *Evil* spirits are not mentioned as such, but their existence is implied. What may be the case is that it is Paul who has set these angelic powers against Christ and given them the character of rivals to him, because he cannot tolerate any lasting dualism between good and evil. Then these powers have become only a foil to display the unrivaled excellence and wide embrace of Christ's reconciliation and victory. They are not like the "opposites" in the second-century systems which had a permanent character and were invested with a quasi-metaphysical function.

Our conclusion concerning this part of the error runs as follows. Evidently Paul had to face tendencies and teaching at Colossae that set God and the world in some sort of opposition. God was distanced and made remote; the world was spurned and the human body held in contempt and its physical appetites held on unnaturally tight rein. Possibly some teachers had argued from the premise of a dualism between God and matter that asceticism should be replaced by its opposite. The trend

95

would then flow toward libertinism. If matter has no relation to God (the argument ran), then the material body has no relation to religion. Therefore a person can indulge his or her body without restraint or conscience (cf. the false teaching combated in II Peter 2:4–22; 3:3; Jude 4, 7, 8, 16; I John 3:4–18; and Rev. 2:14, 20). To be sure, there is no explicit reference in this epistle to an antinomian strain leading to license. But it may well be in the background, and if so that would then explain Paul's vehement and stringent moral warnings in 3:5–8.

Conclusion

The soil of Phrygia was fertile ground for the luxuriant germination and growth of strange religious practices as Paul and his colleagues viewed them. The synagogues had a reputation for laxity and openness to speculation drifting in from the Hellenistic world. In the Colossian church we appear to be in touch with a meeting place and melting pot where the freethinking Judaism of the dispersion and the speculative ideas of Greek religion are in close contact. Out of this interchange and fusion comes a syncretism that is both theologically novel (bringing Christ into a hierarchy and a system) and ethically conditioned (advocating a rigorous discipline and an ecstatic visionary reward). On both counts, in Paul's eyes it is a deadly danger to the incipient church, and on both counts it is exposed.

The Place of Paul's Imprisonment

The epistle to the Colossians belongs to a group of Pauline letters known traditionally as the Imprisonment Epistles. The reason for this name is simply the fact that four of the letters give evidence that he was "in bonds" when he wrote: Eph. 3:1; 4:1; 6:20; Col. 4:3, 10, 18; Phil. 1:7, 13, 14; Philem. 1, 9.

Of this collection of four letters, three of them stand together. Colossians 4:7–8 and Eph. 6:21–22 speak of Tychicus as a bearer of the two epistles, and there are indications of "the most extensive verbal contact" between the two letters at this point (so Dibelius-Greeven, on Eph. 6:21-22). Moreover, Tychicus had as his companion on the journey to the Lycus valley Onesimus, who is mentioned in the note to Philemon as returning at what is presumably the same time (Philem. 12). So this "covering letter" is brought into the same orbit as Colossians-Ephesians. The place of Archippus adds a

96

confirming feature. He is addressed in Col. 4:17 and also in the list of recipients (in Philem. 2). On the other hand, there is nothing in Philippians that suggests a dating at the time of these epistles, if we are to judge from the memoranda of proper names and travel plans.

A further observation is of some importance. Paul's future, as reflected in Philippians, was full of uncertainty and anxious foreboding. His life was in the balance (1:20–23, 30; 2:17) and he had no way of predicting which way the decision would go, though he hoped for a release on pastoral (1:24–26) and theological grounds (2:24) rather than trusting to any favorable turn in his legal position as a prisoner. Indeed, on the latter score, he can contemplate his fate as a martyr for Christ (1:21; 2:17).

The other three prison epistles show none of this apprehensiveness and alarm for the future. The tone of Colossians is calm and even; there is nothing to compare with the perturbation of spirit suggested in Philippians. If these two letters belong to the same captivity, we are forced to imagine that Paul's situation worsened considerably in the interval between the two letters, requiring that, if the imprisonment is identified with the one recorded in Acts 28:30, Colossians (but not Philippians) may well belong to the earlier phase of the two-year detention at Rome. This is the traditional view.

Yet this setting of Colossians in Paul's missionary career has been discussed and debated, and the issues can be read in the standard New Testament handbooks. Our inclination is to place the writing of the two letters—to the Colossians and to Philemon—in the so-called Ephesian period of the apostle's ministry. It follows the arguments of those who suggest that this apostolic letter belongs to that tumultuous period of Paul's life, represented in Acts 19—20, when for a brief space his missionary labors were interrupted by an enforced spell as a detainee near Ephesus. Epaphras came to bring him news of troubles on the horizon at Colossae; and our epistle is the reply, as Paul brings the mind of Christ to bear upon a pressing theological and religious issue.

Paul's answer, couched in epistolary form, met a species of false teaching that increasingly in future years was to afflict the church. The Pauline gospel and Greek thought (in a Hellenistic-Jewish dress) were engaged in struggle; and the letter to the Colossians "thus represents the first confrontation of Christian-

97

ity with a trend against which it was to be forced to defend itself for centuries to come" (Klijn, p. 117).

The Question of Authorship

So far we have assumed that the epistle is a genuine composition of Paul, written at his dictation and sent out in his name. This view, of course, does not exclude the possibility that Paul incorporated other material into his letter, and there is considerable evidence to show that 1:15–20 and maybe 2:10–15 had an independent existence as a pre-Pauline hymn that Paul inserted at a crucial part of his letter. We have discussed this probability in the commentary (Cannon has a full discussion, with a different approach offered by Kiley; see Bibliography).

The tradition that Colossians is authentically Pauline stands on good ground (its most recent modern champions are O'Brien and Wright; see Bibliography). The later church fathers accepted it, and there was no dispute over its authorship in the earlier decades. Marcion included it in his canonical list, and it found a place in the Muratorian Canon. The letter itself confirms this, with Paul's name appearing both at the beginning (1:1) and at the end (4:18) of the letter.

In recent times, however, scholars have raised strong and serious doubts about the epistle's coming directly from Paul's hand. The standard introductions will display the reasons for these questionings, on the grounds partly of content and partly of style and word usage. It cannot be said that the evidence points to a certain conclusion, and the present author's persuasion is to stay with Paul's authorial responsibility for the letter, though with some hesitation. Far less hesitation is entertained over the authorship of Ephesians.

Our knowledge of how Paul's letters were composed is limited. This epistle witnesses indirectly to the use of an amanuensis (4:18), but we cannot say whether Paul gave liberty to a secretary (Timothy is Schweizer's nominee) to write up the final letter from his rough draft, taken down by dictation. On that assumption, however, the unusual literary style of the epistle could be explained, along with the presence of some terms not found elsewhere in Paul (some 25 words, on Marxsen's count; Lohse, p. 134, has 28 words listed). These rare words, moreover, are largely technical or quasi-technical terms, which Paul may well have borrowed from his opponents, especially if he is quoting their actual language or using phrases suitable in debate. In addition, he does incorporate the hymnic period (1:15–20) where a proportion of the special vocabulary is found.

The absence of some of the characteristic Pauline stylistic features especially in the use of particles may be set down to the nature of the letter. On this count, W. Bujard comes to diametrically opposite conclusions from those of Percy. The latter (p. 38) appealed to the liturgical-hymnic style expressing prayers and thanksgivings as parallel with the elevated style found in such passages in the uncontested Pauline epistles. On the contrary, Bujard (pp. 231–235) finds the sentence buildup in Colossians to be unparalleled in Paul. While it is a polemical document, it is not written in a combative style, as is Galatians (Gal. 4:20; 5:12). Paul felt keenly his pastoral responsibility for the churches of Galatia (Gal. 1:6; 4:12–20). But the Colossian letter, addressed to a congregation he knew only at a distance, is by contrast more dispassionately reasoned and detached. This special occasion required a specialized vocabulary and gave Paul's scribe a simpler task to compose in a more leisurely, systematic, and reflective style, with his principal less animated and passionate than on other occasions (as when Paul wrote II Corinthians 10—13).

OUTLINE OF THE EPISTLE TO THE COLOSSIANS

Colossians 1:1–2
Opening Salutation

In this opening Paul consciously adopts the stance of his role and authority as a special messenger of the risen Lord. His greeting borrows some conventional literary forms, but the tone is shot through with a Christian flavor and shows his deep sense of the family awareness in the bond that unites him to his "brothers and sisters" in the Lord (NRSV).

There is a close similarity between the first line of this letter and the introduction to II Corinthians. In both cases Paul is laying claim to his apostleship as a special messenger of Christ Jesus. The basis for such a claim is found in the phrase "by the will of God" (also in Eph. 1:1). But the writer here goes on to associate Timothy as his "brother" with himself, though he does not extend to his colleague the title of "apostle." One distinction may be noted. There is no evidence that Paul's apostolic standing had been challenged at Colossae as it was at Corinth (see later on v. 24, however). Yet in both epistles the apostle found it needful to defend his teaching from rival versions; and this polemic stance is tacitly affirmed by the claim to be regarded as a valid representative of the heavenly Lord (reasserted in vv. 23, 27–29).

Timothy's name is included most probably because Paul wished to identify a coworker evidently known in the Asian churches and to answer an implied criticism that he was simply expressing his own ideas. Perhaps too Timothy acted as a secretary in writing the letter, leaving Paul to take over at 4:18 to inscribe his own signature.

In place of the (to us, expected) mention of "church" at Colossae, the writer expresses the same idea with several powerfully descriptive phrases, namely, "the saints and faithful brothers and sisters in Christ" (NRSV). This translation is preferable to one that makes the wording express two qualities of the Christian family member, that is, "the holy and faithful brethren." The Colossian believers as "the holy ones" recalls Israel's destiny as God's elect people (see on Eph. 1:1, but there is nothing in Ephesians comparable to Col. 1:12, where "holy ones" are the angels) and the extension of that calling now to include the people of the new Israel, both Jewish and Gentile. There is, however, no explicit theological rationale as in Eph. 2:11–22. The quality of fidelity is especially meaningful in view of the calls to steadfastness in the face of encroaching teaching (v. 23; 2:6–7).

The greetings of "grace" and "peace" show that the conventional forms of salutation, expressed by the colorless verb *chairein* (as in James 1:1; cf. Acts 15:23, 29; 23:26), could be reminted to carry the rich freight of the Christian key word "grace" *(charis)* and expanded to pick up the supreme blessing of men and women in the Old Testament world. "Peace" (Heb. *shālōm*) announces the arrival of the new age of God's favor and the human experience of salvation in its widest outreach and application.

Colossians 1:3–8
Reasons for Thankfulness

Paul's prayers strike the note of thanks to God for his readers—their faith and fidelity. He rejoices with them because of their Christian standing and the evidence of their faith seen in the practical expression of their lives and works. In the recording of his prayers it was Paul's literary style to express thanks to God in the preamble of his letters, a convention borrowed from contemporary letter-writing habits but enriched by his distinctively Christian convictions.

One other feature of his opening thanksgivings is the way he found occasion to congratulate his readers and establish friendly relations with them. Pseudo-Demetrius, *On Style,* marks this as a praiseworthy device in good letter-writing conventions. To this may be added the result of some recent scholarly work on New Testament letters to the effect that in the opening themes of the apostle's thanks to God the epistolary situation of the following letter is outlined and described. So here the writer's gratitude for his readers' firm and growing faith is also a tacit call for them to remain loyal to the apostolic message that (in this instance) his representative, Epaphras, has brought to them (v. 7).

Paul did not know this congregation at firsthand. His knowledge came in reports that reached him from Epaphras (v. 8). The substance of that news was altogether heartening as Paul proceeds to pay tribute to the Colossians' faith, love, and hope. This triad of virtues recalls the formula in I Cor. 13:13, which is arguably pre-Pauline as a compendium of Christian moral qualities referred to in several places (I Thess. 1:3; 5:8; Rom. 5:1–5; Gal. 5:5–6; Eph. 1:15, 18; 4:2–5; Heb. 6:10–12; 10:22–24; I Peter 1:3–8, 21, 22; *Barnabas* 1:4; 11:8; Polycarp, *Philippians* 3:2–3). It looks as if the threefold form of terms thought to be essential to Christian experience is used neatly to sum up what Epaphras relayed to Paul in prison on his return from Colossae. The historical allusion to "the day you heard and understood the grace of God in truth" is to Epaphras's mission preaching at Colossae (4:12–13) when Paul sent out traveling preachers into Asia (Acts 19:10). Paul had a high regard for his colleague, designated "our dear fellow-servant" (NEB). He was also a native Colossian (4:12).

Colossians 1:9–11
Paul's Prayer

The apostle's prayers are full of meaning, far removed from glib sentiments ("God bless you!") and superficial wishes. The prayers enter into the readers' situation and lift the mind to see that situation in the light of God's purpose for the church.

Yet another historical notice (v. 9) sets the stage. When news came to him that as a result of Epaphras's initial evangelism the Colossians had responded well, Paul was gladdened and expressed his joy in his prayers (v. 3).

The section 1:9–11 gives the content of his pastoral prayer, based on the report of verses 6–8. Many of the thoughts in the earlier section (e.g., "bearing fruit and growing") are picked up in the prayer speech of the later verses.

The main components of Paul's prayer idiom are listed as "knowledge," "wisdom," and "understanding." It is a likely conjecture that these are the exact terms drawn from the teachers who had invaded the Colossian assembly. Paul is evidently aware of their "beguiling speech" (2:4). His strategy to warn against it is interesting. He apparently has taken over the very terms used and disinfected them by his own additional qualification, drawn from his Old Testament Jewish tradition. Thus "knowledge" is not something secret or esoteric but related to the practical business of knowing and doing God's will (see, e.g., Jer. 22:16). The other two terms are qualified by the adjective "spiritual," which is not courtesy reference but a direct appeal to the Holy Spirit whose help is invoked to make it a valid prayer request. "Wisdom" stands in the Old Testament Jewish tradition of obedience to God's way in practical affairs (Job 28:12–28), just as "understanding" speaks of perception when moral choices are to be registered. Moreover, these spiritual qualities are part of the believer's desire to please God in the whole range of life's activities, not just the religious or sacred. Even when hardships ensue and there is opposition, "endurance" and "patience" are needful attitudes for which prayer is made. It is characteristic of the author who wrote Gal. 5:22–23 (the fruit of the Spirit) to add in the note of "joy" and to celebrate, with a return to the theme of thanksgiving (v. 12), the mighty acts of God in redemption and liberation, leading to incorporation in the new age of God's kingdom-in-Christ (I Cor. 15:25–28).

Colossians 1:12–20
Christian Experience and the Christian's Lord

At first glance it is possible to read verse 12 as if the prayer of the previous section were continuing in an expression of thanks to God on behalf of the readers, or even that he is calling for a thankful spirit to abound in them (NEB marg.). But neither impression is correct. If the prayer ended with thanksgiving, it would be a feature unique to Paul's recorded prayers (II Cor.

1:11 is no real exception). Instead, verse 12 is best seen as the beginning of a new section with the words "giving thanks to the Father" having the force of an imperative call to the readers.

This grammatical observation is of some consequence and has played an important role in interpreting the following section. It is the mainstay in the novel proposal of Ernst Käsemann (see Bibliography) that at verse 12 an early Christian baptismal liturgy opens, and we are invited to overhear some of the main sentiments of that service which celebrates the realities of Christian experience. In particular these are *(a)* the share believers now enjoy in the heavenly world ("the saints in light" are evidently the angels whose role as mediators was much discussed at Colossae, according to 2:18); *(b)* the rescue from the satanic realm, where evil powers hold sway (Luke 22:53) and have control (Acts 26:18) that ushers believers into another realm, the kingdom of God's dear son (a veiled allusion to the title associated with Jesus' baptism, Mark 1:11, etc.); and *(c)* the present experience of redemption which is no physical change or automatic process, as Gnostic teachers were to claim, but a moral transformation based on the forgiveness of sins. Being forgiven, in this letter, commits Christians to take up the same gracious attitude toward others as God also has done to them (3:13).

In other words, almost every term in the recital of Christian experience in verses 12–14 is loaded with polemic and designed to counter current ideas of the rival teachers at Colossae. Paul will clinch the rebuttal in a way that is familiar to us from other places in his writing, namely, by appealing to an accepted piece of church teaching, usually cast in hymnic and/or creedal form. That is exactly what 1:15–20 contains: a confessional hymn directed to the cosmic and reconciling work of the Redeemer who has made the readers' experience a reality.

The Christ hymn of verses 15–20 carries all the marks of a poetic composition that can be appreciated even in translation. There are stylistic peculiarities such as the repetition of words and phrases in verses 16 and 20; the presence of identical words (e.g., "first-born" in vv. 15 and 18) coming in the same place in what look to be separate stanzas; the use of constructions such as clauses beginning with "for" in verses 16 and 19 to explain the preceding statements; and the incorporating of the formula "from . . . through . . . to" (as in Rom. 11:33–35) which has parallels in Stoic praises to the deities—all these data show that we are reading a piece of carefully composed writing, set in poetic mold and designed to be read (or sung) as a self-contained whole, not as a series of unrelated statements. Notice too that the readers who figure so prominently in 1:12–14 and reappear in 1:21–23 are singularly absent from the intervening period. This is a clear sign that 1:15–20 is a preformed hymn stitched into the fabric of pastoral discussion and easily detachable.

Modern studies of the Christ hymn are legion and highly technical (see the commentaries, especially Lohse, Schweizer, and O'Brien, with an attempt to put these scholars' works into readable English in Martin, *Reconciliation,* chap. 7). We must refer to these other commentators for a fuller exegesis which will repay the effort. One conclusion emerging from modern study, however, presses for inclusion in our survey. It is a growing consensus that 1:15–20 is both pre-Pauline (mainly because there are a dozen or so non-Pauline expressions and many of the hymn's ideas are not attested elsewhere in the apostle's other writings) and has been worked over by Paul, who has edited what was originally composed as a tribute to the cosmic Lordship of Christ (and perhaps cherished as such in the Colossian church by those whom Paul regarded as dangerously near to betraying his authentic gospel) to give the hymn a new twist. This conclusion of there being two drafts of the hymn may appear to be quite speculative (but there are some good grounds for it; see the commentaries) and unnecessary (but it is a supposition that comes importantly to the aid of the exegete and the preacher, as we shall see).

In order to clarify, let us set down the hymn in lines and strophes, with brackets to mark off the suggested Pauline additions, supplied by way of corrective.

COLOSSIANS 1:15–20

Strophe I

v. 15   (He) is the image of the invisible God,
      The firstborn over all creation;

v. 16   For in him all things were created, both in heaven and
      on earth
      [Visible and invisible,

105

Whether thrones or dominions,
Or principalities or authorities]
All things were created through him and for him.

Strophe II

v. 17   He is before all things,
And in him all things cohere;

v. 18*a*   And he is the head of the body [the church];

Strophe III

v. 18*b*   (He) is the beginning,
The firstborn from the dead
[In order that he might be preeminent in all things]

v. 19   For in him all the fullness was pleased to reside,

v. 20   And through him, to reconcile all things to himself,
Whether things on earth or in heaven
[So effecting peace by the blood of his cross].

The four parts that are bracketed contain elements that cannot be fitted into an arrangement of three three-line strophes with rhythmical and metrical agreement, and seem to be added to orient the hymn in the direction of the false teachers at Colossae. They were evidently giving prominence to the cosmic "powers" (2:8, 18, 20) as independent agents to be venerated in their own right. Paul wants to enrich the hymn's lines to show how all the powers fall within the sphere of Christ's creative work, so their independent existence and authority are debunked.

Note too that the adding of "the church" to verse 18*a* turns the direction of the hymn into new channels. By this token Paul has changed an original tribute to Christ as lord of the world into a statement praising him as the head of the body, now identified as the church. So Christ's body is no longer confused with the physical world. The notion that Christ as the risen one fills the universe with his power and so brings heaven and earth together in a physical way (roughly parallel with Eph. 1:10, 21–23; 4:10) seems implicit in the earlier version of the hymn. Paul's criticism of that Hellenistic idea of wisdom or logos or Zeus filling all things is seen in his corrective adjustment to verse 18. He has done this—lifting the original cosmological tribute onto the plane of ecclesiology as the church's place under Christ's universal authority is spelled out explicitly—in order to assert the preeminence of Christ the risen Lord over his people (as in 2:10; 3:11) as well as over the created orders.

Verse 20 is perhaps the crucial text where this kind of redactional theory has much to contribute to exegesis and proclamation. The global reconciliation of all creation (in the first draft, which lacked the allusion to "making peace by the blood of his cross") has to be understood as a statement of cosmic harmony, endorsing the affirmation, given out in verse 16, that creation is at one with its creator. But this requires a curious nuance to be read into "reconcile," a point to which N. Kehl (p. 41 n. 32) has perceptively called attention. He asks, How can a universe that is already united to Christ as its "head" (v. 18a) stand in need of reconciliation? The answer must be in a different sense given to the verb "reconcile" in that original version of the hymn which Paul has adapted and changed by his significant addendum of verse 20c and so paving the way for an extended application of "reconciliation" to his readers' situation in 1:21–23.

Paul has thereby confronted the situation at Colossae. He has given to the *stoicheia* (2:8, 20), the elemental forces of the universe, a changed status. Like his Colossian readers, he believed that such cosmic agents owed their being to the creator Christ, but when they are brought into a cosmological system and treated as rivals to Christ they stand in dualistic tension with the Christ of Paul's basic monotheism. They take on a demonic character and require him to assume that they have broken away from their station as "created orders" by claiming an independent status, demanding human allegiance and veneration (as 2:18 implies). No longer do such cosmic forces remain neutral as part of the creation; they are in rebellion and need to be "re-created" by having their hostility drawn and neutralized.

The engagement between Christ and the powers took place at the cross, as 2:15 will dramatize. But the victory is his, hence the powers are defeated and Christ's reconciliation involves their subjugation and submission (Phil. 2:9–11). The force of this announcement, however problematic for us to handle, had for Paul immense practical and pastoral consequences. Indeed, he can glide easily from a statement of Christ's deed on the cross to the way it impinges directly on his readers (1:21–23). Indeed,

107

that is the basis of his appeal as he reasoned back from Christ's benefits in human experience (referred to in the frontispiece of the hymn in 1:12–14 and elaborated in 1:21–23) to the more speculative teaching contained in the hymn. Notice that he has brought the hymn into line with his theology by his editorializing additions and has clarified the primary meaning of reconciliation as the restoration of personal relationships based on moral issues, not speculative theory. Specifically he has changed a piece of cosmological tribute into a song of praise to the crucified Lord as an expression of his *theologia crucis* for which Christ's triumph is never seen as swallowing up and extinguishing the cross as the locus of divine power and the inspiration of all Christian worship. It is by the cross that forgiveness of sins is offered (classically stated in II Cor. 5:18–21; Rom. 5:1–10) and true reconciliation is enjoyed.

If our approach to 1:15–20 in the context of its surrounding verses is near the mark, it permits us to see why Paul cited the hymn in the first place (because it was "current coin" in Colossian worship and had possibly been exploited by the teachers Paul wrote to expose), the changes he felt impelled to make to get across his message in rebuttal, and the appeal he constantly makes to Christian experience, arguing from solution to problem, from known realities to theoretical considerations. Once we have grasped these hermeneutical ideas, our understanding and communication of the stately hymn will be better informed. It may help us to address the crucial issues raised by the hymn as we seek to interpret it:

1. Who is the church's Lord? He shares the divine being as the visible representation and manifestation of who God is (so Lightfoot in interpreting "image of the invisible God"). He is not a copy or likeness of God but the "projection" of God on the canvas of our humanity and the embodiment of the divine in the world of men and women (thus Masson on 1:15).

"Christ in creation" (1:15–17) raises the question of his relationship to the universe. Both Jewish and Greek thinkers had ideas of wisdom or logos as the instrument by which the world came into being (e.g., Prov. 8:30 and the Stoics) and by which it was sustained. But no philosopher ever thought of wisdom/ logos as the goal of creation as verse 16 announces. And, for Paul, no part of the universe is excluded (v. 16).

Speculative Greeks did apparently imagine Zeus as the head or ruler of creation (cf. v. 18a), but it seems clear that

Paul's agreement with this tribute to the cosmic Christ is quickly tempered to bring the church on to the scene. That leads to the second major part of the hymn (vv. 18b–20), with verses 17–18a functioning as a hinge to clamp together the two panels (strophe I: vv. 15–16; strophe II: vv. 18b–20).

2. What is the church? is the question posed in the section, verses 18b–20. The twin terms "the beginning" and "the first-born from the dead" clearly celebrate the triumph of the cosmic Lord who embodies the divine "fullness." God's plan is worked out through him whose resurrection and exaltation mark the new beginning of world history. He is the agent in bringing the universe into harmony with the divine purpose, expressed as reconciliation (v. 20).

A couple of indicators, however, give an extra dimension to this Christology, with the recall that just as a head needs a body, so Christ is not considered without his people. The associated terms in verse 18b point back to Gen. 49:3 in the Greek Bible which runs: "Reuben, you are my *first-born,* my strength and the *beginning* of my children" and uses the same Greek words as our text. This combination suggests that the firstborn and risen one, for Paul's hymn, is the founder of a new people (as in Rom. 8:29). If this is a small exegetical point, we would get the reminder of the way Christ is associated with the figure of Adam, who begins the Bible's story. Adam was made to reflect the divine image (Gen. 1:26–27) as God's son and king of paradise. He was the beginning of the old order, doomed to sin, death, and decay. Christ is the second Adam, whose coming marks a new start to world history and the creation of a new race. Moreover, it is over this new segment of humanity, called the church, that he is meant to be pre-eminent (v. 18c), with the reason supplied that "in him all the fullness of God was pleased to dwell," that is, God in his total essence is expressed only in Christ, according to this hymn, and not scattered throughout the universe, as was evidently a current notion ventilated at Colossae (see 2:8–10, where the application to the readers as church is clearly made). The theme of reconciliation by the cross equally has the church in its sights, since Christ's death, vividly portrayed by the reference to his sacrificial "blood," has meaning only as it speaks of God's provision for sinners, assuring them of pardon and a restoration of friendly relations as the basis for reconciliation. To this topic the text will lead on naturally in verses 21–23.

109

In conclusion, Paul is pressing into service a hymnic confession of faith, perhaps originally cosmological in its purport and later edited by him to make it conform to his purpose, which was known and used by the Colossian congregation. It may have been part of their baptismal liturgy which proclaims the Christian's entrance upon new life through obedience to the cosmic Lord as a heavenly eon. The significant thing is what Paul does with the hymn, both by adapting it to set forth a theology of the cross and using its baptismal teaching to recall his readers to the apostolic faith in the sole supremacy of Christ and his present victory over all the spiritual powers (2:10, 15, 20).

Colossians 1:21–23
Application to the Readers

The pronoun "and you" (v. 21) stands in an emphatic position in Paul's Greek sentence as in the RSV translation. There is a close link with the foregoing, as though Paul wished to make it clear that Christ's universal, cosmic reconciliation also—or perhaps mainly—had a personal application to the Colossian readers. Indeed, as Schweizer remarks, that is Paul's point in appealing to the hymn, namely, to insist that reconciliation must not be thought of in terms of physical or metaphysical events which guarantee salvation in an impersonal way. Rather, reconciliation for Paul has meaning only in terms of moral relationships.

That evaluation is worth pondering in a day when a modern version of Christian salvation is offered as either a type of religious science appealing to the curious-minded (New Age religion) or as experience inalienably guaranteed and certified as a once-for-all transaction, regardless of subsequent conduct on the part of the believer. This short paragraph is timely with its reminders of both human needs ("estranged and hostile in mind," "doing evil deeds") and human destiny, to be "holy and blameless and irreproachable" in God's eyes. The latter are terms drawn from the Old Testament whether ceremonial (Exod. 29:37–38) or eschatological, promising that at the judgment day no sentence of condemnation will be brought against God's people. Either way, it is a character transformation that is promised, provided the elect people remain faithful and morally sensitive (v. 23).

Fidelity is to be directed principally, in this context, to Paul's message. So it is fitting that Paul's ministry is brought to the fore and held up for acclaim. He is known as its "servant" (Gr. *diakonos*), a term shared by Epaphras (1:7) and Tychicus (4:7), both of whom needed to be reinforced and commended at Colossae. They are part of Paul's team ministry, and trustworthy.

Colossians 1:24—2:5
Paul's Ministry to the Churches

This longish section is really dominated by a single theme. Quite likely Paul—or his colleagues mentioned above—had to defend his ministry against insinuations at Colossae that his sufferings showed that his claims to leadership were doubtful; in any case, his absence as an apostle in jail (4:18) needed some explanation to those who may have wondered why he did not arrive at Colossae to present his teachings. There is clearly a polemical thrust to what follows, culminating in a plain warning at 2:4. The entire section, then, is a sustained statement of "apology" in which Paul seeks to show how integral his work is, as a divine commission, to the full discharge of God's saving plan among the Gentile churches. His strategy is *(a)* to give a rationale for his sufferings; *(b)* to comment on his ministry as designed to herald the inclusion of the non-Jews within the scope of God's saving purpose, much as in Rom. 11:13; and *(c)* to sound a call to his readers to be on their guard, a call from one whose interest in them, although they were not directly founded by his ministry, is solicitous and all-embracing.

Paul writes, above all, a word of encouragement (2:1) even if he is on the defensive and feels the need to account for certain circumstances, notably that he is a prisoner and known to be a constant companion of "afflictions" (II Cor. 11:23–28) and that he is unknown personally at Colossae as elsewhere in the cities of the Lycus valley. As ever, Paul's justification of his ministry is set within a theological frame. He has taken this opportunity, although constrained by pastoral pressures, to remind the read-

111

ers of the leading themes of his message (1:26–27), of the tenor of his ministry with its threefold responsibility and task ("proclaim . . . warning . . . teaching," 1:28) and of his seriousness at all times (1:29—2:1) to achieve his goal. That goal is to present "every one" (three times repeated, as though to hint at the inclusiveness of his concern) "mature" (Gr. *teleios*, perhaps a watchword bandied about at Colossae, where it may have been used of being initiated to the cult of 2:18). For Paul, maturity is found "in Christ," that is, in union with him and obedience to his will (2:6–7). It implies here a determination not to be carried away to strange notions and fall victim to seductive speech (2:4). The Pauline mandate calls the readers to clear-sighted apprehension of the truth of the gospel (1:23; 2:2) and a resolution not to break ranks as the apostle sees himself (in 2:5) as an army commander standing before his troops and reviewing the parade (so Lohmeyer). "Good order" and "firmness" are terms drawn from the military academy.

So far the section is clear. The one reference that causes some exegetical trouble is 1:24. The afflictions Paul endured are well known, and he needs to explain that they were not because he was a foolhardy person who loved to live dangerously and take risks as a piece of machismo. The key phrase is "for your sake," that is, Paul is the suffering apostle on account of his calling as apostle to the Gentiles (Eph. 3:1, 13). He complicates matters by going on to write about "in my flesh [his mortal existence, as II Cor. 7:5; Phil. 1:22] I complete what is lacking in Christ's afflictions for the sake of his body, that is, the church." A parallel passage is II Cor. 1:5–7, and in both instances the most likely idea is taken from the Jewish apocalyptic teaching that Israel's chosen ones will have to suffer a quota of afflictions before Messiah comes. Paul takes over this concept of vicarious suffering and bends it to his purpose. In his life of service to the Gentile congregations he is called upon to represent his people as a martyr figure and to perform a vicarious ministry on their behalf. In this way he fills up the still deficient tally of sufferings that God's new Israel has to endure before the end of the age.

Colossians 2:6–9; 2:10–15
Paul Confronts the Situation at Colossae and Responds

Although Paul's confidence in the Colossian church's soundness and support of him is mirrored in verse 5, it does not prevent him from addressing it in terms of advice (vv. 6–7) and caution (v. 8). He could not take for granted their continuance in the faith, and it is this salutary yet pastoral concern that moves him.

The appeal to tradition opens his remarks here. In a wise manner he harks back to the early days of the Christian mission at Colossae ("just as you were taught" recalls just that), and he is able to renew confidence in the authentic and sincere response they gave to the ministry of Epaphras (1:6–7). Several metaphors illumine the type of reaction Paul gratefully acknowledges: rooted (as a tree sends down strong roots into the soil); built up (as a house takes shape in gradual construction); and established (a legal term, speaking of a contract that is ratified and made binding). So the readers are invited to reflect on their initial pledges of faith by which their community life as believers was begun.

Yet if there is the genuine Pauline tradition, conveyed by Epaphras as a trusted servant of the Lord (4:12), a rival tradition has posed a threat and the Colossians must be on their guard lest anyone should "kidnap" them (2:8) and carry them off as a prize of war. He puts his finger exactly on the nature of this teaching, "according to human tradition." It is identified by two pejorative remarks: it is a philosophy which Paul regards as a hollow sham, and it gave inordinate place to "the elemental spirits of the universe" (see Introduction for what this term may connote). The severest judgment brought against this theosophical system is that it set up a rival allegiance to Christ, either by demoting him to an inferior place in the *plērōma* (the fullness) or by insisting that his was not the sole mediatorship between God and the world (v. 18). It is needful for Paul evidently to rebut this assertion, and it is pastorally, as well as theologically, important to see how he does so.

113

The following subsection (2:10–15) offers the outline of the apostle's response, but while we can trace the main thrust of his counterteaching, he has left several unresolved and puzzling matters to tease our minds, notably: What is Christ's circumcision (v. 11)? What is the certificate whose charge is leveled at us (v. 14)? And how did the crucified Lord deal with human plight in a superhuman engagement with cosmic agents and spirit powers (v. 15)? The academic commentaries should be consulted for an array of suggestions as to the possible answers. It must suffice for us here to observe the lines Paul took in coping with a menacing situation about which all we really know is what he tells us, or which we may infer from his responses. Perhaps, however, it is more to the immediate point if we look at the way he approaches the threat.

First, there is a forthright affirmation of what he took to be cardinal Christian truth, that is, in Christ (and so not in the cosmic powers) the whole fullness (not a part) of deity dwells bodily (in Jesus' human person, not in a cipher or make-believe humanity which is a mere cloak for deity, so Schweizer). All of this in verse 9 sets the stage for what comes later, and is fundamental to it. Christ's sharing in the life of God is not at the expense of his equal share in our humanity, so that the classical doctrine of the incarnation is neither a piece of adoptionism by which a good man is taken up into deity nor a charade by which the earthly Jesus was only God role-playing as man. The fullness of the godhead came to live in a truly human life which was lived out in our world as the perfect "image of God" in a human person (1:15).

Second, the movement from Christology to soteriology (in v. 10) is to be closely observed. It is Paul's essential position that the teaching on Christ's person and achievement is directly related to its effect on the world and the church; in other words, the Christology is functional, not speculative. Having established the point that the divine essence in its totality resides in Christ, Paul moves quickly to show the result in the way his readers came to benefit. They have come to "fullness of life" in him. Melanchthon's dictum is well spoken: to know Christ is to know his benefits.

The third move in Paul's thinking unpacks how he thought the "fullness of life" came to the readers. In simple terms, he is directing attention to such memorable experiences of the Colossians' life as baptism (vv. 11-12), new life in a spiritual awakening from death (v. 13), forgiveness and a fresh standing before God (v. 14) because Christ the victor overcame all their enemies and accusers (v. 15). So much seems clear. It is when we press the details that our exegetical troubles begin.

I suggest that the key phrase lies in verse 11: "by putting off the body of the flesh" (NRSV). This is, at first glance, Paul's idiom for recalling the Christian's initiation to new life in Christ. The noun translated "putting off" (Gr. *apekdysis*) suggests a clean break with a past life, though the precise metaphor is one of disrobing and stripping off a set of clothes preparatory to taking on a fresh wardrobe (as in 3:9–10). What is in view is the baptismal act when new converts divested themselves of their ordinary clothes for baptism and reclothed themselves after the rite (see Gal. 3:27, and the early baptismal liturgies such as the *Apostolic Tradition* of Hippolytus of Rome, ca. 215 C.E.).

The link with circumcision is fairly obvious, since for the apostle the steps to membership in the old covenant community (requiring the physical operation) are transformed into what is needed to enter the new covenant in Christ, that is, a shedding of old allegiances, certified in baptism, which is the counterpart to Old Testament Jewish circumcision. In the baptism it is God's work ("a circumcision made without hands") to initiate the new life of obedience to the heavenly Lord (see Lohse). This is likened to a resurrection and a new beginning to one's relationship with God (v. 13), of which the most vivid experience evidently was the assurance of pardon and liberation from all evil powers.

Such a line of reasoning is eminently straightforward and attractive, but it may be too simple. If "the circumcision of Christ" (v. 11) means "the circumcision which Christ himself underwent" (see Moule), then a new face is put on the text. It implies that on the cross Christ divested himself of the evil powers that to that point had successfully engineered his death and defeat. Looking on to verse 15, we see that this is exactly Paul's rationale of the cross. There, he "stripped off" (Gr. *apekdysamenos*, akin to v. 11) the principalities and powers that clung to him in an attempt to hold him captive (I Cor. 2:6–8). He did so by stripping off his "flesh," since it was his flesh (i.e., his frail humanity) that the evil powers assaulted. In so doing, he released himself from their control, and—here an abrupt change of metaphor—made a public disgrace of them, as he led them in a triumphal procession as a defeated foe. Here Paul blends a historical illustration and a mythological concept. Vic-

115

torious Roman generals paraded their captives of war in chains through the streets of the city at the conclusion of a foreign campaign. The "enemy" in Paul's scenario are the demonic powers that are in rebellion against God and implacably hostile to the church. They are exposed to ridicule in the seeming defeat of the cross. In the hour when they appear to have won the day, Christ turned tables on them and they are themselves carried off as his prize of war (perhaps going back to the verb in v. 8).

Finally, the last-mentioned cross-reference, even if it is a guesswork, points us in the direction of Paul's purpose in erecting such a dramatic stage setting for the event of Good Friday. His interest is chiefly pastoral and polemical. Hence verse 14 with its allusion to the certificate that was "against us" has to be read in the light of 2:20–21. There it refers to the teachers' ritualistic prescriptions imposed on the Colossians. Paul meets in advance the insistence on these taboos, and he does so by pointing to the cross where (in the scenario of 2:11–15) Christ's achievement was to take that IOU (which is what the Gr. *cheirographon* means; Philem. 18–19) brought against humanity by evil spirits and pay the debt. He did so by identifying himself with the sinful race (Rom. 8:3; II Cor. 5:21; Gal. 3:13) and dying for humanity's plight. So Christians share in that accomplishment and freedom as they accept "the circumcision of Christ" which not only forgives their past sinfulness but sets them free from thralldom to evil and in particular releases them from false negative religion. To this application Paul will come in 2:20–23.

Paul calls into play a vivid imagination in order to reassure his Colossian friends that no matter how strong the forces of evil arrayed against them may be and no matter how insistent the false teachers may be that they are helpless victims of spirit powers (which need to be placated: see 2:18), Christ is supreme. All cosmic forces are subject to his Lordship. In that sense they are "reconciled" (1:20), with their hostility pacified and their power to hurt neutered. More dramatically still, these cosmic and malevolent powers are exposed to disgrace and made a laughingstock. In a passage of deadly stern tone, Paul ends tellingly with a note of parody, with a tongue-in-cheek rebuttal.

Note on Demystifying the Powers

It is commonplace that we do not and cannot share the powerful fear of Paul's contemporaries that principalities and powers reign in the upper air, that the stars exercise a malign influence, or that personal demonic forces contaminate food and drink (anticipating what will be said in 2:20–23). The question is whether Paul also saw the demonic powers as so much superstition from which Christ came to set men and women free. His thinking seems to have oscillated between a recognition that demons "do not exist" (I Cor. 8:4; this sentence may well be a quotation from the Corinthians themselves) and an admission that their influence is baneful and must be resisted (I Cor. 10:19–21). Certainly the writing in Colossians belongs to the latter category, with special emphasis on Christ's triumph and rule (2:15).

One way in which we can translate Paul's confidence in Christ's victory over the spiritual powers is offered by F. F. Bruce (*Paul: Apostle of the Heart Set Free,* pp. 422-423; see too Stewart, pp. 420–436). He appeals to the lure of astrology and the occult in modern society which, in spite of its confidence in technocracy and claim to sophistication, is often plagued by superstition and the spell of age-old taboos. There are also powerful socioeconomic and political forces that are raised to the level of demonic structures (see Berkhof, *Christ and the Powers,* and Wink, *Naming the Powers,* but Lincoln, *Ephesians,* is critical of Wink's approach on exegetical grounds) against which we as individuals and in society struggle often in vain. Atomic physics and electronic gadgetry have spawned a complex system of weapons and data-recording controls that threaten either to obliterate human life on the planet or to submerge the individual in a sea of serial numbers and algebraic codes. Deep-seated fear and psychoses threaten our mental stability and stand in the way of our attaining "fullness of life."

The hermeneutical knot is thus deftly severed by this appeal to "demythologizing" or perhaps de-demonizing. Paul has used language, to us archaic and "old world," which is capable of being transposed to fit a new idiom in our symbolic universe and to speak to a modern scene. The lords which govern the planetary spheres are debunked by Paul "to stand for all the forces in the universe opposed to Christ and his people" (Bruce).

Given the legitimacy of this transfer, we have inherited from Paul the basic confidence that no force in the world— "demonic" or human, impersonal or personal, structural or individualistic—can separate us from God's love in Christ (Rom.

8:39). The key to the mysteries of the cosmos as well as the ills, tragedies, contrarieties, and perversities of our human lot is offered in what Paul regarded as a major component of his "gospel," namely, Christ's oneness with humanity in its lostness and alienation and his victory—in which we are invited to share—over all cosmic/superhuman powers that are inimical to humankind as God's creatures and children.

Colossians 2:16–23
Defense of Christian Liberty

The intention of this passage is essentially practical, in spite of appearances that suggest the presence of some strange teachings (vv. 18, 23): to establish the practical consequences of "living life in its fullness" under Christ's Lordship (see v. 10). That is why we have chosen Masson's heading "Defense of Christian Liberty" to sum up. The terminology and the ideas it expresses about Christ's person and work, stated in 2:8–15, are seen to have their repercussions at the practical level. Paul is proceeding to show the folly of any course of action based on wrong theological premises. He opened the discussion (at v. 8) by denouncing "philosophy" and "empty deceit," which stand in diametrical opposition to Christ. Now he will level an even more damaging criticism against these teachers who are "bursting with the futile conceit of worldly minds" (v. 18, NEB). The root of the problem is their failure to hold to Christ as the head (v. 19). And from that lapse Paul draws the conclusion that their ethical principles are worthless, since those principles are no better than "human precepts and doctrines" (v. 22) and emanate from "self-made religion" (v. 23). The writer thus gives a "blow-by-blow rebuttal of their pretentious claims" (Lohse).

At first glance the way verse 16 highlights the prescriptions belonging to an ascetic manner of life seems to point to Jewish customs. The teaching that Paul opposes and warns the Colossians about looks simply to be part of dietary restrictions and the celebration of sacred days and festivals in Judaism, whether mainline or sectarian. As far back as 1875 Lightfoot referred to the example of the Essenes, a monkish community in the Judean desert, who practiced a type of asceticism and separatism.

118

Our knowledge of this protest group has been greatly enriched by the discovery of the Dead Sea scrolls and the community at Qumran that followed a lot of these rules. Yet it is too simple to think that Paul's opponents were Jewish teachers, as we shall see from verse 18. The Greek term for "law" *(nomos)* is strikingly absent from the entire letter, a fact that makes it very unlikely that Paul's problems are the same as at Galatia where he takes on the Judaizers.

The contrast of shadow/substance is a Platonic one, suggesting that the "real" world is mirrored in what we see and that we need to press behind outer appearances to be in touch with reality. Perhaps the readers were insisting that "full reality" (what they called *plērōma*) could not be attained except by way of venerating the angels, who were being regarded as the "copy" or mirror image of the divine, and by obeying their ascetic regimen as a route to this goal. If so, Paul turns the tables on them by giving a christological twist to the contrast. The essence of reality, its substance (lit., "body"), is Christ. Here is the nub of the debate, then; and it is the touchstone by which the apostolic teaching tests and evaluates all rival claims to an attainment of reality in religion. To lose touch with Christ is to miss one's way (v. 19); to remain in communion with him is the key to life in its totality (*plērōma*, 2:10).

We may follow recent studies in noting that the flow of the argument starts with a report of what the rival teaching was advocating (see especially Francis and the modern commentators: see Bibliography). First, how access to the divine was promoted is described (v. 18); then, how the ascetic life was to be maintained (vv. 21–23). But Paul is not content simply to report and describe, he interspersed critical comment with a view to denunciation and correction. The fact that these criticisms are interwoven does not make for easy comprehension, but we must make an effort.

The Colossian "philosophy" aimed to enrich Pauline teaching by "insistence" (a strong term) that *(a)* bodily denials and rigorism in matters of diet and sexual celibacy (v. 21, "Do not handle" may be a term for curbing the human libido) were needful in order to attain to God. *(b)* "Worship of angels," meaning either the veneration paid to them or (less likely) the worship the angels conducted or practiced, meant that access to God was possible only by their mediatorship. *(c)* In order to enter the divine presence and be initiated as a worshiper or

119

devotee (v. 18, a rare term rendered "taking his stand on visions," RSV, but better, "going into detail about what a person sees in a trance"), one must adopt a set procedure, requiring fasting (v. 18, "abasement" means just that) and an ascetic preparation.

The flip side of the teachers' program has to do with "regulations" (v. 20). This reference repeats what was said earlier about abstemiousness in food and drink and reinforces it. The key word is "rigor of devotion" (v. 23) which sets a puzzle for the translators. It is evidently a term that Paul borrowed from the Colossian teachers if the prefix *ethelo-* (which is akin to the participle *thelōn,* "insisting" in v. 18) betokens their pleasure in advocating a religious outlook and practice expressed in terms of asceticism and self-denial. They hope that, once their regimen is followed, and their spell is cast over the Colossians, the result will be self-mastery and a visionary experience that will be far superior and more satisfying than anything the Pauline gospel has to offer. That evidently was their claim, and on face value it looked attractive. It smacked of novelty and excitement; it promised a trancelike ecstasy that lifted the devotee onto a higher plane of experience; and it pandered to an innate human desire to be part of an exclusive set, a cut above the rest, and a "super Christian" (see pp. 87–90 under "The Threat to Faith and the Colossian Crisis" in the Introduction to Colossians).

Paul will have none of these claims and their supporting arguments. In particular he brings the following charges of indictment against the philosophers and cultists.

1. They are mistaken in their bid to gain access to the divine by dreamlike visions, since they turn away from Christ, the true image of the invisible God (1:15). They are thereby severed from him (2:19).

2. Their veneration of the angelic powers overlooks the role of these beings as created (1:16) and subservient to God who has revealed himself finally in his son as preeminent mediator for the church (1:18).

3. Since Christ is the victorious head and the spirit world is under his dominion, any bid to live by regarding the angels as intercessors is to put the clock back—or, to use Paul's own expression, to remain in the shadows when the sun is at high noon (v. 17).

4. Negative religion never satisfies whatever it may claim to

120

do (v. 21). It leaves unchecked our passions and untouched our real problem which is not with our instinctual drives but with our motives. These latter are prey to our selfish desires, the Pauline "flesh" (v. 23), and can be reoriented to noble ends only by a radical transformation *from within,* not by any external code or prohibitions (the "regulations" of v. 20).

5. Finally, from Paul's perspective is the exposing of human pride. The so-called "abasement" (vv. 18, 23) lamentably fails in its objective simply because if it were to succeed in producing what it promises, the result would be only to make men and women proud of their attainment. Their "sensuous mind" (v. 18; lit., "mind of the flesh") yields only a desire to be on a religious pedestal and is a form of one-upmanship, that is, I am better than the rest and have reached a pinnacle by my own effort. The next step is to despise others less favored. The outcome, for Paul, is the very antithesis of true humility, movingly set forth in 3:12 as a quality of true life in Christ and in fellowship with one's brothers and sisters in him.

So with the bridge section (3:1–4) which epitomizes the destiny and privilege of being risen with Christ, Paul will proceed to a statement of true self-denial.

Colossians 3:1–4
Lift Up Your Hearts

The call to enter into Christian liberty has two sides. At 2:20 the emphasis is negative: "If with Christ you died. . . ." But Paul, who opposed all life-denying taboos and restrictions in 2:21–22, is not content to remain with that negative statement. He moves on to the natural complement: "If then you have been raised with Christ. . . ." In both instances he is assuming that his readers have indeed participated (presumably in their baptism) in those life-enhancing experiences.

Now comes the application. "Seek" implies the orientation of a person's will either to an unprofitable goal (Rom. 10:3; I Cor. 1:22) or to a worthwhile end (Rom. 2:7). He directs the readers here to "things that are above," perhaps in conscious opposition to "earthly things" (Phil. 3:19). But the immediate referent is to the claim that secret knowledge of heavenly reali-

121

ties may be gained by close investigation (2:18; the Gr. verbs in both 2:18 and 3:1 may carry this sense: see Greeven in *TDNT,* 2:893).

This entire subsection may well be determined by its function as a way of celebrating Christ's exaltation as the basis for the church's new life. No longer are believers held captive to the spirit powers; they are bidden to share in the triumph and enthronement of their Lord whose future reign is, to be sure, an anticipated event (v. 4). These emphases are held in some tension, expressed by the dictum "now . . . not yet," that is, Christians in the Pauline congregations were taught that their salvation was a present reality, yet at the same time its fulfillment and perfection lies in the future, "when Christ who is our life appears" (see I Cor. 15:20–28).

Colossians 3:5–11
True Self-Denial

Once more we are in touch with the positive aspects of Paul's moral theology. He has already found fault with the stifling negativism of the rival teaching (2:20–23); it is time to accentuate the positive (beginning 3:12), while as a preliminary he must insist that his moral teaching is opposed to indulgence (3:5–9), since it is based on life in the new order (3:10–11).

Paul's drastic summons, "Kill off" (v. 5), has chiefly sexual sins in its sight. The list ranges from extra-marital relations to gross immorality seen in sexual excess and perversion (Rom. 1:26; I Cor. 6:9; cf. Eph. 5:5). "Covetousness" stands out as the last member of the list. It breaks the sequence by turning attention from sexual vices to greed as a species of materialism. The normal meaning of "covetousness" (Gr. *pleonexia;* lit., "a desire to have more," the *amor sceleratus habendi,* the "accursed love of getting" described by Roman moralists) is an insatiable desire to possess. Quickly goods become our gods. So the equation with idolatry is apposite. Yet a sexual overtone for "covetousness" is also found in I Thess. 4:6.

122 Either way, whether the noun relates to *libido inexplebilis* of which Cicero wrote or the materialistic outlook, it is a painfully obvious trait of the human condition in every age and culture. The vivid description of Shakespeare:

> The cloyed will,
> That satiate yet unsatisfied desire, that tub
> Both fill'd and running.
> *Cymbeline* 1.6

rings true in modern Western society with its lust for instant pleasure and concern for an ever-expanding consumer market. The "wrath of God" comes on such a culture in many ways.

The contrast of "then . . . now" referring to the readers' pre- and post-conversion days lies at the heart of much Pauline ethical exhortation and is seen in verses 7–8. They are reminded of what life in the old order (v. 9) was like. They are summoned by that reminder to take on the characteristics of the new society in which they have found a place (v. 10) as God's creation, renewed and being transformed in the church where "Christ is all" (he is the key to new life, 2:10) and "in all" (he is to be seen in all his members whose common life in Christ transcends what separates them on the ground of ethnic status, religious affiliation, cultural difference, and social condition, v. 11). This is an exciting paragraph with a relevance and topicality for the preacher-teacher which is not far to seek.

Its timeliness comes out in yet one other way. The sins set out in serial form (vv. 8–9) all have to do with the human power of speech. The age-old question, What is man? permits many answers, some frivolous (as Samuel Johnson discovered when he quoted an ancient philosopher's definition as a "two-legged animal without feathers" and his rival promptly had a cock plucked bare), some facetious (like Johnson's own attempt: man is an animal that cooks its food), and some serious. Among the most thoughtful is the description of a human being as a speaking animal *(homo loquens)*. Among the species, the human being stands alone in commanding the power to use words to communicate ideas, to express personality, and to enter into dialogue. The power of the tongue is a distinctive feature of the human race and carries with it all manner of effects, good and ill alike, as James 3:6–12 well exemplifies.

In the new creation, begun in Christ, there is no room for sins of speech that are so destructive and hurtful. The range is impressive, from outburst of anger and uncontrolled temper to crude talk and "economy with the truth," bluntly named (v. 9) lying. Christians at Colossae are to regard this way of life as finished, since as they recall their baptism they are to allow its dynamic effect to release them and to act out their baptismal profession of being true to it. They will become in actual fact—

123

by their renunciation of the old life and acceptance of the new, given them as they were raised with Christ—what they were declared to be in their baptism.

This, in a nutshell, is Paul's basis for ethics. It seems far removed from the simple exhortation that today often passes for Christian teaching in the pulpit, namely, Follow Jesus and do your best. We should set against that simplistic (and often futile) advice, however well intentioned, the robust Pauline insistences. They run on these lines.

Paul harks back to the Colossians' decisive, life-changing entry into God's kingdom (1:13) when they shared in Christ's stripping off from himself the alien tyranny of demonic powers (2:11, 15). That event in question was their baptism (2:12, 13, 20) which inaugurated in union with Christ the Lord their Christian standing (3:1, 3). Moreover, the old nature once abandoned and the new nature now assumed are essentially corporate terms for membership in two kingdoms (1:13), akin to the Old Testament Jewish polarities of "this age/the age to come." For Paul, the symbolic universe is set out as "in Adam/in Christ," with Gen. 1:26–27 clearly in the background of our text. Becoming a Christian, for Paul, was nothing short of leaving the old order (in Adam) and being taken up into the new eon determined by Christ's advent as the last Adam. This is the new creation of II Cor. 5:17, and it is membership in a new world. But the old order (Gal. 1:4) still persists and presses its claims. These must be refused—until the end comes when the present kingly authority of Christ will be caught up into God's eternal rule (I Cor. 15:20–28). In this interim the church lives as a signpost pointing to its final destiny but embodying now what God intended human life-in-society to be (v. 11; cf. Gal. 3:28; I Cor. 12:13).

Colossians 3:12–17
Christian Distinctives

Paul's set of ethical principles, expressed in the contrast "put off . . . put on" (3:8–10), may have seemed too abstract and/or idealistic for the readers. He proceeds, therefore, to make the appeal more specific and down-to-earth. There are virtues to be cultivated (v. 12); how Christians will react to certain human situations when their equilibrium is upset (v. 13) follows; and love is the typically Pauline badge of the Christian profession (v. 14). Let us note the switch from the excessively negative and theoretical tenor of the previous section, with its calls, "Put to death," "Put away," "Put off"—all part of Christian catechism that has aptly been labeled *Deponentes,* that is, lay on one side, and have done with, referring to old ways of conduct. Now the accent falls on the more life-affirming stance, appropriate to the readers' destiny as God's chosen ones whose life is to mirror the divine character (the Old Testament allusions in the words of v. 12 are given in most commentaries; they are part of one facet of Judeo-Christian paraenesis, namely, the imitation of God; cf. Matt. 5:48).

Peacemaking attitudes are a natural accompaniment of this life-style. "Forbearing" and "forgiving" go hand in hand (v. 13). Love is praised in I Corinthians 13 as the cardinal virtue; here it plays a picturesque function as the knot that ties together the other graces and so gives a coherence to Christian living by supplying a drive force and motive. The goal is a "perfection," viewed as "perfect harmony" (NRSV) or an integrative whole with no part out of place or lacking.

Certain "steps" to the attainment of this goal are spelled out in what follows. The phrase "in one body" reminds us that the horizon of thought is the life of the church in society. To give a social expression of their identity Christians are called first into "peace with God" through Christ (Rom. 5:1) and then into a peace-creating society as they display Christ's lordship and judgeship ("rule" means to arbitrate, to give a verdict, as in a legal case or an athletic contest; cf. Wisd. Sol. 10:12: "in his arduous contest [wisdom] gave him the victory," that is, decided in his favor).

Christ's "word"—in this context, Paul's message to be cherished and heeded in the face of alien ideas of false wisdom (2:23)—has its setting in a worship service that opens with the call to thanksgiving (v. 15c). As the letter is read out in a public gathering in some house congregation (Nympha's at Laodicea, 4:15–16, as well as Philemon's in Colossae, Philem. 2), these exhortations will take on special significance, urging the people to encourage one another by words of (true) wisdom, that is, Pauline teaching as well as vocal praises. Early hymn-singing activities evidently covered a wide range of material drawn

125

from the Old Testament Psalter, Christ songs like the one in 1:15–20, baptismal chants as in Eph. 5:14, and ecstatic/charismatic hymnody (I Cor. 14:15, 26). The ministry of teaching and instruction was now set in this liturgical framework; it was by such poetic creations, inspired by the Spirit, that the believers were consolidated and given the weapons to defend their faith. The idea of "hymns" as teaching vehicles in early Christianity is a recent one (see Hengel, pp. 173–197, and Martin, "New Testament Hymns," pp. 123–135), with topical relevance; it puts a question mark against much "free" worship with pitiably weak, sentimental, and introspective chorus/song singing in some churches today.

The final reminder is intended to catch up the whole of life—not just its Sunday exercises—and place it under the aegis of the Lordship of Christ (v. 17). Worship takes on its true character as "a living sacrifice" (Rom. 12:1) when it is viewed as setting the agenda for what Christians do in the world and the spirit in which they fulfill their calling as servants of God. Both the mystical strain of George Herbert ("Teach me, my God and King, / In all things thee to see") and the robust evangelical fervor of Charles Wesley ("Forth in thy name, O Lord, I go / My daily labor to pursue") join hands at this point.

Colossians 3:18—4:1
Family and Social Duties

The flow of thought moves on to consider how the general principles, given out in 3:17, are to be worked out in specific situations. The call to "Do everything in the name of the Lord Jesus" is an umbrella challenge intended to cover all facets of life. Now Paul spells out in some detail the relevance of this rubric to social concerns. The readers live in a particular network of social relations and will need to see the applicability of the apostle's teaching to themselves. It is interesting that Paul draws on some accepted instruction to enforce his point, evidently with the desire to make plain that this was the quality of corporate life expected in his communities. It is not simply his own way of looking at life or admonishing others.

Several sections of the New Testament run parallel with

126

this passage (3:18—4:1), namely, Eph. 5:22—6:9; I Tim. 2:8–15; 6:1–2; Titus 2:1–10; I Peter 2:13—3:7. In varying ways, all address practical counsels to husbands, wives, children, masters, or slaves. They draw on maxims found in Hellenistic popular philosophy, especially of Stoic origin. The best designation of these "rules," sometimes referred to (after Luther) as "household tables" *(Haustafeln),* is station codes, that is, Christians are addressed according to their relation in life and society and especially within the Christian household. The party is named, a command or prohibition is given, and a motivation for behavior is supplied (see Lillie, pp. 179–183). The key idea in these examples is submission, though there is a reciprocity between the members (Eph. 5:21) not found outside the New Testament in contemporary writings. The primary motive behind the admonitions is that such an attitude expresses subordination to Christ's Lordship, which is (naturally) a distinctively Christian component.

As to background, there are many suggestions (tabulated and discussed in my "Haustafeln," in *NIDNTT,* 3:928–932) ranging from the origin of such teaching in Stoic circles and transplanted to early Christianity to the influence of Hellenistic Jewish missionary outreach to Gentiles who were required, on conversion to Judaism, to accept basic moral and social values for the ordering of life. James E. Crouch (see Bibliography) has probably the best solution when he argues that, whatever their origin (which he finds in the link between the Greek appeal to fundamental "unwritten laws" and rabbinic insistence on elementary morals, avoiding immorality and idolatry), the Pauline rules, which are christianized as they are taken over, served a teaching function. They were designed to impose a check, in the face of incipient lax morality as Paul's charter of freedom (Gal. 3:27–29) was misunderstood and all restraint cast off. They led to a safeguarding of the social fabric, partly on the theological ground that God's creation ordinances (in marriage and the family) are good and partly on the pragmatic level which requires that the Christians are not at liberty to overturn the social-political-economic framework of society by revolutionary means or feminist independence. If this is a reasonable way of viewing the role of the station codes, it will explain why Col. 3:18—4:1 (the first example on record of this genre of writing) appears the way it does and why it is restrained and tempered in its solutions. All of them are conditioned by the existing

127

structures of first-century society in which the church lived out its corporate life.

The calls follow this pattern. Wives are summoned to be "subordinate" (i.e., to keep their place in the social order, to honor marriage as then understood, and to act as Christian believers). There is no theological development or rationale, such as is given later in Eph. 5:22–33, as a basis for the corresponding appeal to the husbands. Children were regarded in low esteem in Greco-Roman society (see the Stoic epitome of Hierocles, second century C.E., 4.25.53, in Malherbe: children contribute to their parents' joy by performing even seemingly servile duties such as washing their feet, making their beds, and standing ready to wait on them). We may note how strikingly modern is the Pauline word to acknowledge that they do have "rights" (v. 21). Moule rightly regards this as opening a new chapter in social history.

Slavery was endemic in the ancient world. The slaves propped up the social order by their sheer strength of numbers but were regarded (at least theoretically) as no better than "a thing, a living property" (Aristotle, *Politics* 1.2.4–5, 1253b) or a "living tool." They had no legal rights, and their basic freedoms, notably to work where they chose and to move freely, were denied. True, not all slavery was debasing and painful, since slaves managed households, ran businesses for their masters, and did secretarial duty as well as toiled in the mine and the galley. Yet slavery did impose an essential loss of liberty. There is no hint in the New Testament that slavery is morally wrong. Rather, the lines of evidence assume that the social conventions and their economic support in slavery will remain in force. In place of any summons to revolt (rather, "stay in your station" is Paul's advice, I Cor. 7:17–24), the exhortation is to be honest and hardworking (cf. Philem. 18 for Onesimus's failure here, on the usual interpretation: see commentary later), to be encouraged by future recognition on the part of the heavenly master whose service on earth is what really counts, and to do one's daily chores as an expression of Christian vocation. Nor are the slave owners left out of the picture. They are told to be fair and scrupulous in their dealings, with the reminder that they too (as believers) live under the eye of God (4:1) and so are subordinate to God.

128

If this tone of advice seems pedestrian and accommodating, we should respect the limitations of what could be said in urging both slaves and owners to maintain the social order. The incitement to revolt would have been suicidal, as the earlier slave uprisings, led by Spartacus in 73–71 B.C.E., had shown. Paul's last word on how slavery was to be fitted into a christianized cell in society is heard in his note to Philemon.

Colossians 4:2–6
Exhortations and Appeals

A wider angle of vision is now opened, as Paul turns to invite his readers to prayer and gracious behavior, especially winsome speech. The general call to prayer (v. 2), coupled with warnings to alertness (because the Parousia is near? see *TDNT*, 2:338) and a reminder of the duty of thankfulness (a frequent note in the letter; 1:2; 2:7; 3:15, 17), is followed by the writer's own request (v. 3).

The "mystery of Christ" (v. 3), which is the subject of the apostolic proclamation (1:26; 2:2), is viewed here as the reason for Paul's imprisonment and at the same time the occasion to invite his readers to share with him in seeking an "open door" of release from confinement. The metaphor is one Paul used elsewhere (I Cor. 16:9; II Cor. 2:12) and illustrates the apostle's desire to see his mission extended through the world (as 1:23 reports as a past event). The intention is slightly polemical. In contrast to the narrow exclusiveness of the rival philosophy, the Pauline mandate reaches out to embrace all.

"Wisdom" was evidently a much-debated concept at Colossae. Paul takes over the chameleon-like word and gives it a fresh content as being a human response to God's will (1:9, 28) and also a life-style in the world informed by following Christ, God's incarnate wisdom (2:3) and instruction (3:16). Part of that way of life was the ability to give a reasoned defense of the faith, but always with an attractive presentation, a point akin to the emphasis in I Peter 3:15.

Colossians 4:7–18
Plans and Greetings

The time has come to draw the letter to a close. The transmission of the letter is entrusted to the hands of Tychicus, Paul's confidant. He will amplify what is sent in written form by word-of-mouth news of the apostle's whereabouts and living conditions. More important, no doubt, Tychicus (a Pauline travel companion, according to Acts 20:4, and a visitor to Ephesus, according to II Tim. 4:12) is the partner in this task with Onesimus, who with Paul and his master Philemon is one of the chief characters in the letter addressed to Philemon. He had come to be with Paul either as a fellow prisoner (so Winter: see Bibliography on Philemon) or, more likely, as a new fellow believer who sought refuge in Paul's company.

"Fellow prisoner" may be a metaphorical term for sharing with the apostle in the bonds of Christ, as the phrase "in Christ Jesus," used of Epaphras in Philemon 23 and of Paul in Eph. 3:1; 4:1 implies. This description fits Aristarchus in verse 10. Aristarchus is known from Acts 27:2 as a companion of Paul's in later life. A man of Macedonia (Acts 20:4; 27:2), he accompanied Paul on his visits to Asia (Acts 19:29; 20:4), thus giving him a link with the Lycus valley churches. He also may have connections with the collection for the Jerusalem saints, if he is concealed in the paragraph of II Cor. 8:18–22.

John Mark is a less shadowy figure on the stage of apostolic history. He is recommended in a way that suggests he is only slowly regaining his reputation (after the lapse recorded in Acts 13:5, 13; 15:36–41?). Hence the identification with Barnabas's family circle. Mark's mother was evidently well known in Jerusalem (Acts 12:12, 25), and tradition links him with Peter and the writing of the second Gospel, which bears his name. Later New Testament tradition connects him warmly with Paul (II Tim. 4:11). Among a group of Jewish Christians including Mark the name of "Jesus called Justus" stands out.

It is pleasing to note Paul's tribute to these Jewish Christians, especially as his attitude toward this group in II Cor. 11:4,

13–15 is implacably hostile. The former group evidently took a non-proselytizing attitude toward the law and/or circumcision and perhaps represent a type of Jewish Christianity reflected in the letter of James in which the Torah is a boundary marker of identity but not a badge of ritual observance for salvation (as in Phil. 3:2–3 and Galatians).

The Colossians knew these names, we assume. Certainly they would be cognizant of Epaphras. He was "one of your-selves" and delegated to visit Paul (1:7) with news of the church (1:8–9; 2:5). Now he is commended as a leader who, at a distance (since he shared Paul's confinement, Philem. 23), still remembers the congregation and has accepted a responsibility to pray which is both serious and strenuous. He apparently took the other churches of the Lycus valley beneath his aegis (v. 13). The reference to "assurance" belongs to the warp of the letter (1:9, 19; 2:9–10) and represents a felt need among a people disturbed by alien teaching that must have unsettled them (1:23). The antidote lies not in the offer of "maturity," being perfect (Gr. *teleios*), nor in gnosis, but in adherence to the apostle's teaching of true wisdom in Christ (1:28; 2:3).

A final cluster of names rounds off the greetings list. All the characters have their own importance for early Christianity: Luke, Paul's fellow worker (Philem. 24) and sometimes re-garded as Paul's attending physician, certainly a medical person whom tradition connects with Antioch; Demas, whose epitaph is written in II Tim. 4:10 but who at this time (Philem. 24) is still on the honor roll; Nympha, a woman's name according to most modern editors of the text in verse 15, who opened her home to the church gathering, as was common practice (Philem. 2; Acts 16:15, 40; Rom. 16:5, 23).

The letter to the Laodiceans, thence to be passed on as "the letter from Laodicea," is lost for reasons we can only guess. Was it lost in the earthquake of 60 C.E., as P. N. Harrison (see Bibliog-raphy) thought? Was it destroyed or suppressed when the church lost its Christian character (Rev. 3:14–22)? Does it sur-vive in the (canonical) letter to the Ephesians, as in Marcion's list, or in the apocryphal letter that goes under that name? Is it a lost letter, written by Epaphras and so discarded because it did not originate from a well-known author? Who can tell? We don't know.

The ministry of Archippus (v. 17) is again an unknown quan-tity. He evidently belonged to the family of Philemon (Philem.

2) and has some pastoral responsibility at Colossae, which he may have been tempted to take lightly. Perhaps, as John Knox (see Bibliography) opined, he is being encouraged to see to the release of Onesimus from servitude on his return to his former owner who is usually (and clearly) identified with Philemon. The theory that makes Archippus the master of Onesimus is not very cogent, as we shall see. More likely the diaconate of Archippus has to do with his task in keeping the church together, a rather daunting responsibility in the face of the problems exposed by the letter.

Paul now takes the stylus from the hand of the scribe who, like Tertius in Rom. 16:22, has been wielding it, and he appends his own signature. It is a mark of authenticity and a final appeal to heed his teaching. The recall of his chains is no piece of sentiment and dramatics. Paul holds up his manacled wrists to impress the readers with his authority as a suffering apostle. Not pathos but authority is the sign he points to by his chains, and what the call seeks to elicit is acknowledgment and obedience, not sympathy. Yet the last word is spoken with the tender tones of grace, with which the epistle opened (1:2) and by which the church at Colossae—or wherever, in all ages—lives.

THE BOOK OF
Philemon

Introduction

Introducing Philemon

The part of the New Testament that goes under the name of Paul's letter to Philemon has a special, if unusual, claim on the attention of all students and preachers of Paul. It carries all the marks of a personal note, addressed to a friend and his circle whom Paul speaks of in terms of endearment and affection. Its theme is the release of a slave from punishment and a recommendation that he not only should be treated with forgiveness but should be given a welcome into the Christian family as a cherished family member.

It is surprising that the church would want to retain this simple appeal and incorporate it into its library of what later was regarded as sacred Scripture. The truth is that Paul's advocacy of the slave's case was genuinely revolutionary and marks the opening of a new chapter in social relationships. The letter speaks about how the members of Christ's church are to relate to one another and treat one another. Hence the letter has this timeless significance, even if some details are matter for scholarly debate. A knowledge of some first-century customs is, then, in order.

The Occasion and Purpose of the Letter

This is the shortest of the letters that go to make up the Pauline corpus, consisting of 335 words in the original Greek. It is the only example in the extant Pauline correspondence of what may be termed a personal note, although recent writers have drawn attention to the way in which the letter opens, associating Timothy with Paul and associating with Philemon the whole church which assembles in his house. They take these details to mean that the document is an "epistle" (i.e., a document intended for a public hearing). This is confirmed by verse 9 in which the translation "Paul, an ambassador" (Gr. *presbytēs*) is to be preferred to "Paul, an old man." In short, this brief epistle is to be seen not so much as a private letter of Paul as an individual but as an apostolic letter about a personal matter or as John Knox (p. 59) expresses it: "a letter to a church, embodying (would we say 'enclosing'?) a letter to an individual." But it still remains true that the individual in question (Philemon) is seen as a member of the corporate fellowship of Christians all of whom have an interest in his decision.

The study of Norman R. Petersen (p. 69) draws attention to the central literary problem in the letter. He identifies two kinds of sequence. There is a referential sequence of actions, telling a story *about* Paul; a poetic sequence is the description he gives to the letter *to* Philemon. The two sequences overlap, or run together in parallelism, as his table (slightly modified) will show:

THE REFERENTIAL AND POETIC SEQUENCES OF ACTIONS IN THE LETTER TO PHILEMON

Chronological Steps	Referential Sequence	Poetic Sequence
1 (v. 19*b*)	Philemon incurs a debt to Paul	5 (vv. 4–7)
2 (v. 9; cf. vv. 1, 10, 13, 23)	Paul is imprisoned	2 (v. 9)
3 (vv. 15; cf. vv. 11–13 and 18–19*a*)	Onesimus runs away and incurs a debt to Philemon	———
4 (v. 10; cf. v. 13)	Onesimus is converted by an imprisoned Paul	4 (v. 10)
5 (vv. 4–7)	Paul hears of Philemon's love and faith	———

Chronological Steps	Referential Sequence	Poetic Sequence
6 (v. 12)	Paul sends Onesimus back to Philemon	6 (v. 12)
———	———	3 (v. 15)
7 (vv. 17–19*a*)	Paul sends a letter of appeal to Philemon and offers to repay Onesimus's debt	7 (vv. 17–19*a*)
———	———	1 (v. 19*b*)
8 (implied)	Onesimus and the letter arrive	8 (implied)
9 (vv. 20–21)	Philemon responds to Paul's appeal	9 (vv. 20–21)
10 (v. 22)	Paul's anticipated visit to Philemon	10 (v. 22)

The occasion of the letter may be inferred from its contents even though some details are obscure. A slave named Onesimus had wronged his owner Philemon, who was a Christian living at Colossae (vv. 1–2; cf. Col. 4:9, 17 with Archippus named in the prescript), and had run off. Onesimus had in some way come into contact with Paul, either as a fellow prisoner or because he had sought refuge in Paul's company. In the latter event, it has been proposed that he could have benefited from Athenian law by which a runaway slave could seek asylum in the home of a friend at the family altar (see Goodenough, pp. 181–183) or from Jewish law (Deut. 23:15–16: so Derrett, pp. 63–91). The first provision was widespread throughout the empire, and it may throw some light on Onesimus's desire to seek Paul's protection, though it is difficult to explain verse 13 in view of the further requirement that a delinquent slave must be sold if he refused to return to his former owner.

The nature of the slave's offense is not certain. It is usually assumed that he had stolen money and then absconded (v. 18). But as Roman law required that whoever gave hospitality to a runaway slave was liable to the slave's master for the value of each day's work lost, it may be that Paul's promise to stand

135

guarantor (v. 19) is no more than the assurance to Philemon that he will make up the amount incurred by Onesimus's absence from work. For this background, see the fragmentary papyrus (Grenfell and Hunt, pp. 70–72) dated 298 C.E. The entire note, as reconstructed and translated by the editors, is worth quoting in full:

> Aurelius Sarapammon, called Didymus . . . to Aurelius. . . . I appoint you by this my instruction as my representative to journey to the most illustrious Alexandria and search for my slave called . . . aged about 35 years, with whom you too are acquainted . . .; and when you find him you are to deliver him up, having the same powers as I should have myself, if present, to . . . imprison him, chastise him, and to make an accusation before the proper authorities against those who harbored him, and demand satisfaction.

It may be that the slave had come on an errand to Paul and had overstayed his time. At all events, the primary purpose of the letter is to act as a covering note to ensure that Philemon will receive back his delinquent slave, although some scholars (Winter, pp. 1–15) regard the injunction of Paul to Philemon as a request that he was asking Onesimus to be returned and allowed permanently to remain as his aide. This has been criticized (by Derrett, p. 64). Verse 21, however, does contain an undertone of hope that Philemon will agree to the manumission of the slave. The various methods by which a slave could gain his freedom were as familiar as the institution itself. It was common for the slave to deposit money in a temple and for the god and his priests to officiate in the transference as his freedom was purchased. But for forgiveness to be shown to a criminal slave who had escaped was another matter. Paul's plea was a revolutionary thought in contrast with the contemporary treatment of runaway slaves whom the master could take steps to arrest and then brutally punish. Compare the wording in Oxyrhynchus papyrus 1643 (quoted above): "you shall imprison him and whip him." The master could even have the slave crucified. A surviving papyrus dated in the mid-second century B.C.E. gives the text of a warrant for the arrest of a slave on the run. Rewards are offered to any person who finds him and brings him back or who can give information as to his whereabouts (e.g., in the temple of a god whose protection he has sought [seeking manumission?]). An even higher reward is promised to an informant who says that the slave is lodging with a private person; then not only would the slave be returned but the

person who harbored him could be prosecuted and held liable
for the loss of the slave's work incurred by his absence from his
master.

Paul's bold request for Onesimus is therefore carefully prepared for by his use of gentle language (vv. 8–9) with its tones
of entreaty and leads to an appeal to Philemon's willing cooperation and consent (v. 14) and the promise to accept any liability
that he may have incurred (v. 19).

Yet the letter does not stay on the surface of a simple request for a slave's life on humane grounds. A good illustration
of a plea for clemency on a humanitarian level is seen in the
younger Pliny's letters to a certain Sabinianus (*Letters* ix. 21,
24). He intercedes for a young freedman who has sought refuge
in Pliny's home and is full of fear at the prospect of his master's
wrath. Pliny grants the master's right to be angry but tries to
steer Sabinianus in the direction of clemency (Lat. *mansuetudo,*
a Stoic virtue) because of the deserter's repentance, amend-
ment of life, and request to be forgiven. Sabinianus is entreated
to be benevolent and to forbear his anger, which has been justly
aroused. The tenor of Pliny's letter is quite different from
Paul's, and the contents are obviously not the same. Paul says
nothing about Philemon's "rights" to exact vengeance, nor does
he even contemplate that Onesimus will be punished.

Running through Paul's appeal is the current of Christian
compassion (v. 12) and the powerful reminder that Philemon is
already in debt to Paul himself (v. 19*b*) as owing to Paul's
preaching of the gospel his very salvation under God. The characteristic notes are therefore: "for love's sake" (v. 9), "refresh
my heart in Christ" (by acceding to this request, v. 20), and
receive this truant slave "as you would receive me" (v. 17). The
request ends with a parting shot (v. 21) that Philemon will go
beyond the limit of Paul's desire; this appeal is reinforced by the
prospect of the apostle's visit (v. 22), a hope that would spur
Philemon to a ready acceptance of what was asked of him.
There is every reason to believe that he did respond; otherwise
the letter would not have been preserved at Colossae.

The Place of Origin and Date

Paul writes as a prisoner (vv. 1, 9, 10, 23), and a careful
comparison will show that this letter was sent from the same
place as the Colossian epistle. Onesimus is to accompany Tychicus, who was entrusted with the Colossian letter (Col. 4:9).
Moreover, Paul's situation as a prisoner may well have drawn

137

Onesimus into his company; some scholars believe that Onesimus had been caught and placed in the same cell as the Christian missionary and so won for Christ. But this can only be speculative.

The placing of this epistle in a suitable period of Paul's life adds very little to our knowledge of either the letter or Paul's mind. The close tie between the letters to Philemon and the Colossians is a datum that all interpreters accept (save for some exceptions, e.g., Goodenough, p. 182 n. 7, who does not think that the Onesimus of Philemon is the same as the man referred to in Col. 4:9, and Haenchen, p. 474 n. 1, who questions whether the Mark of Philemon 24 is the John Mark of Acts 15:37, as Colossians 4:10 assumes). It follows that if the case for a dating of Colossians in the Ephesian period of Paul's ministry is preferred, this will virtually decide the issue in respect of Philemon.

The Historical and Pastoral Significance of the Letter

As a historical document, the letter throws unusual light on the Christian conscience against a background of the institution of slavery in the ancient world and so complements and corrects what we find in the so-called "rules of the household" *(Haustafeln)* of the other New Testament epistles (see esp. Col. 3:22—4:1; Eph. 6:5–9; cf. I Cor. 7:21–23; I Tim. 6:1–2; Titus 2:9–10; I Peter 2:18–21). From these traditional teaching patterns Paul draws the framework of his instruction, but he injects a moral tone with his reminders that the slaves are "serving Christ," that the owner has a "master in heaven," God who deals impartially, and that both slave and owner are bond servants of Christ. From that last position it is a short step to a relativizing of slavery which in turn reaches the point at which it becomes indifferent (I Cor. 7:20–24) and has lost its sting (Gal. 3:28; Col. 3:11)—at least, insofar as slaves and masters are members of the one household of Christian faith.

The question is sometimes raised that the New Testament never condemns slavery explicitly and so it is defective at a crucial point. Yet part of the answer to this implied criticism is that Paul does not advocate a social philosophy that countenances revolution and violence. In the exigencies of the social structures of the Roman Empire of Paul's day, slavery could be 138 overthrown only by violent means; and the apostle will be no party to class hatred or violent methods (cf. Rom. 12:17–21). Cf. *Diognetus* 7.4: "Coercion is incompatible with God."

Further, Paul's whole approach to Philemon is voluntaristic, leaving Philemon to settle the matter by appealing to his conscience. "The real problem of the letter is not Onesimus' slavery but Philemon's freedom," to use M.-A. Chevallier's provocative words, cited in R. Lehrmann (p. 9). Though Paul could order him to act, he prefers to allow Philemon to respond with a measure of spontaneity and self-determination. What matters to Paul is to secure Philemon's willing consent, not in perfunctory compliance but because he sees his duty as Paul wishes him to see it. It is this feature, represented in both Paul's attitude toward Onesimus as a "child" and a "brother" (there is no condescending paternalism in Paul's references) and his relations with Philemon as a joint sharer in the Christian faith and experience, which lifts Paul's appeal onto a different level from contemporary humanitarianism seen in Stoicism. Paul bases no conviction on a common humanity shared by slave and master; rather, he writes to a fellow Christian about a slave who is a fellow Christian. He employs a Stoic term in verse 8, "what is required" or "fitting," but quickly modifies it to his own ends.

The note to Philemon, then, while it is ostensibly about the treatment to be given to a law-breaking slave by his master, is more properly thought of as a witness to "life in Christ." The "teaching" it contains is more of how the Christian life is to be lived in a social context. It aims to construct a "network of new situations and the circuit of new relations which constitute the life in Christ, the life of the Church" (Preiss: see Bibliography) and to set the particular issue of Philemon's treatment of Onesimus in that network. The apostolic attitude toward slavery as an institution is nowhere defined and, at best, has to be extrapolated from his teaching on the life of Christian believers.

Note on the Later History of Personalia in Philemon

Another value of this small epistle derives from the important place it holds in the reconstruction of Paul's correspondence adopted by Knox (see Bibliography). Knox offers two identifications that, if accepted, would modify our understanding of this letter and enlarge our picture of apostolic and later Christianity. They are (1) that the real slave owner was Archippus, not Philemon to whom Paul appeals and whose services he seeks to enlist in an attempt to persuade the former to have compassion on Onesimus; and (2) that Onesimus was set free to return as Paul's aide; and he became in due course the bishop of Ephesus in the second century, an identification attested

139

(says Knox) by Ignatius, who in his letter to the Ephesians shows that he had read this epistle to Philemon and actually adopts the same play on words that Paul uses in verse 20. Ignatius writes: "May I always have profit from you [Gr. *onaimēn hymōn*], if I am worthy" (*Ephesians* ii.2). With this identification assumed, Knox proceeds to maintain that the same Onesimus, now a church leader, was responsible for the collection of the Pauline letters and their publication—including the one to Philemon in which he had such a personal stake.

Critical opinion on these two hypotheses has not been too favorable. Moule (pp. 16–17) rightly objects that Philemon's name standing at the head of the list of persons addressed (v. 1) seems "fatal to the theory that Archippus is primarily the one addressed." Further criticisms have fastened on such matters as (1) the use that Knox makes of Col. 4:17 (see commentary). For his reconstruction, this verse plays a significant part in identifying Archippus's "ministry" as that of obeying Paul's recommendation and accepting Onesimus. But this is by no means obvious, since the verb Paul uses, "you fulfill the ministry," is an active word (so Moule) and the service Archippus had "received" is more probably something that had been "handed on" to him by tradition. Moreover, the delicacy of Paul's appeal in the letter to Philemon is lost if he gives a blunt order to the slave owner in Col. 4:17. (2) The inferential nature of the relationship between Philemon and Archippus in which the latter needs to have pressure applied by Philemon is a weakness in the theory, since there is nothing to indicate such a relationship. We must remain content with Dibelius-Greeven's verdict: "Speculation about Archippus' position in Philemon's household is idle." (3) H. Greeven (pp. 373–378) concentrates on Knox's translation of verse 10, which is taken to mean that Paul is asking that Onesimus be permitted to remain (pp. 19–20) and on the identification that Knox makes of the "letter from Laodicea" (Col. 4:16) which is the note to "Philemon." In this "letter from Laodicea" we are meant to see the letter sent first to Philemon who was an overseer of the churches in the Lycus valley and who lived at Laodicea, the main town in the region. Paul wrote to Philemon first of all so that his influence could then be brought to bear on Archippus in Colossae. In this way, it is claimed, we can do full justice to Paul's prepositional phrase: "the letter *from* [Gr. *ek*] Laodicea." But no such meaning is required, and Greeven can produce several reasons why this letter to the Laodiceans has not survived.

F. F. Bruce (pp. 90–92), however, is sympathetic to Knox's second point but unpersuaded by his attempt to give Archippus a distinguished role. He does concede the possibility that the identification of the ex-slave with the Onesimus who is mentioned in the first six chapters of Ignatius's *Letter to the Ephesians* as "a man of inexpressible love and your bishop" (1:3) is correct. Certainly it is a coincidence that this name should turn up in this way. However, it may be that we are stretching the long arm of coincidence too far in making the identification. A more cautious view would be to accept the suggestion of J. B. Lightfoot (pp. 308–309) and think that the later bishop of Ephesus took the name of Paul's friend. Lightfoot mentions another Onesimus to whom Melito, bishop of Sardis half a century later still, dedicated his volume of Old Testament extracts (Eusebius, *Church History* 4.26.13f.). So the practice of revering "Onesimus" by taking his name—perhaps because of its symbolic meaning—is not unique.

Summary

We should not fail to note the value in this epistle of the window it opens into Paul's character. He is the true apostle who is also, as Chrysostom aptly comments, a man, full of sympathy and concern for a person in distress and willing to do all in his power to help, even at some cost (v. 19). Each of the parties involved was called upon to do something difficult: on Paul's part, to deprive himself of Onesimus's service and company; for Onesimus, to return to his master-owner, whom he had wronged; for Philemon, to forgive. "And each of the three [is to do] what he was called upon to do as a Christian" (Scott, p. 59). Moreover, Paul so identifies himself with both the slave and his master that he can fulfill the office of mediator, and represent meaningfully both parties. Our knowledge of Paul would be so much poorer if this slender document had not been preserved.

OUTLINE OF THE EPISTLE TO PHILEMON

Philemon 1–3
Greeting

Paul writes as "a prisoner of Christ Jesus" (NEB), which may mean no more than an expression of commitment to Christ as his servant. But the request for prayer (v. 22) that he may be released suggests rather that he is in captivity (see vv. 9–10). The names of his associates (vv. 23–24) also indicate an imprisonment identical with the one from which he wrote to the Colossians; and he was a prisoner then (Col. 4:3, 18).

The addressees are Philemon and Apphia, who is often taken to be his wife, along with Archippus (known from Col. 4:17). This collocation of names may group the three names into one family. But there is a wider audience as well, as "the church in [Philemon's] house" is included. House congregations were common in early Christianity (see on Col. 4:15). The letter, ostensibly a private note to this family and to Philemon in particular, is intended to be read out in public worship. Hence the "grace and peace" formula, to mark a liturgical salutation.

Philemon 4–7
Thanks and Acknowledgment

The "epistolary situation" is at the heart of this opening period. Paul's prayer of thanks to God will introduce the theme of the letter, as words and ideas, summarily given here, are repeated later: love (vv. 5, 7, 9, 16), prayer (v. 22), a sharing, partnership (v. 17), the good, goodness (v. 14), heart(s) (vv. 12, 20), refreshed (v. 20), and brother (v. 20).

142   Paul's acquaintance with Philemon looks to be distant (v. 5) as he remarks on the way he has learned of the man's response to the message. But a closer bond is indicated later (v. 19), as

Paul recalls that Philemon owed his conversion to the apostle's personal influence.

The aim of Paul's prayer is that his friend's faith may show itself active in what will be the substance of Paul's request later, namely, that he should release the slave and welcome him to the family of God (vv. 15–16). To pave the way for this request Paul pays tribute to Philemon's generosity to other believers as well as the good influence exerted on his own life. Yet the tribute is perhaps more a literary device, since "refresh" will reappear in verse 20 once Philemon has acceded to the apostle's request. The opening section is, then, a type of appeal, based on the importance of establishing a "friendly relationship" (Gr. *philophronēsis*), which Pseudo-Demetrius, *On Style*, says is a mark of good letter writing.

Philemon 8–20
The Request

This paragraph lies at the center of the letter in every way. It brings Paul to the point. Although he might stand on his dignity and use his authority as Christ's agent (lit., "ambassador") to urge Philemon to do the right thing in the light of his Christian faith—namely, to take the slave back with clemency—he chooses, rather, to ground his appeal in love. He is asking for Onesimus's future (v. 10: Knox's and Winter's view that Paul's verb means that he is asking for Onesimus to remain with him seems unnatural [see Bibliography]), which is in serious jeopardy. As a runaway slave, Onesimus was liable to severe punishment, including even death. What Paul is concerned about is the treatment the slave will receive once he goes back to his master.

Onesimus has indeed been with Paul in his captivity, and he proved his worth. The pun on his name (Onesimus = useful) has a dark side, for in his wrong action (v. 18) he has belied the name he carried. Paul pays him the compliment of his present worth, and his help to Paul makes it natural that the apostle would want to retain him. Good relations between Philemon and Paul, however, dictate that Onesimus should go back, but to what kind of welcome?

143

The hidden nuances and deep meanings of this letter are nowhere more evident than in verse 15. To paraphrase Paul's comment: Maybe Onesimus ran away temporarily so that it may be apparent that God's hand was in the episode, for it is divine overruling that in his return he might enter into a permanent relationship with his master, with whom he shares eternal life. But this will come about only as Onesimus's slavery is set on a fresh basis, namely, as a fellow Christian in the household of faith. Paul says no more here than that Onesimus's return should not be punished. At verse 21, he will take the request a step farther and plead for the slave's manumission and release. Yet (at v. 17) Paul hints at a new situation he longs to see emerge. Perhaps its model is that of the Roman partnership contract (*societas,* equaling the Gr. *koinōnon:* so Winter, pp. 11–12). "Receive him as you would receive me" means "give him full acceptance" as a Christian (Rom. 15:7).

His past misdemeanor cannot be ignored, however. Paul wants to have the account settled, as he offers to take full responsibility for all that Onesimus may have stolen. An IOU in Paul's name (cf. Col. 2:14) will guarantee this repayment.

A final reminder of the debt Philemon owes—in a context of incurring debts and making repayments—clinches the point. Philemon is bound to acknowledge his own role as a debtor whose obligation to Paul is tactfully introduced to persuade him (vv. 19*b*–20). "The plot of Paul's story is structured around the theme of indebtedness" (Petersen, p. 291).

Philemon 21–25
Final Remarks and Greetings

Another note is sounded in the mention of "obedience," replacing earlier tones of "entreaty" (vv. 8, 9, 14). Perhaps the obedience sought is to be directed to God, with Paul his agent. Paul is confident that the Colossian slave owner will do what is asked, and even more. No one is sure what this extra entails, whether that Onesimus will be allowed to return to Paul (so Knox and Harrison: see Bibliography) or (more probably) that he will be set free at Colossae. At all events, Paul is extending the request announced earlier (v. 16).

Still with consummate tact (that refuses to issue a mandate, v. 8, but resorts now to a head-on insinuation), Paul announces that he plans to visit Colossae. Then he will see what effect his letter has had. This travel plan is no courtesy gesture but a well-known literary convention to drive home a point (see Doty, pp. 12, 36–37). The appeal for prayer is of the same order.

Final greetings come from personnel known from Col. 4:10–14. All are Paul's fellow workers, an honored title shared by Philemon (v. 2), with the gentle hint that he will do now, as he gets the letter, what the other colleagues would do in the circumstances.

The liturgical "grace" situates the letter in the house congregation at worship.

BIBLIOGRAPHY

Ephesians

1. For Further Study

Barth, Markus. *Ephesians.* 2 vols. Anchor Bible (Garden City, N.Y.: Doubleday & Co., 1974).

Beare, Frank W. "Ephesians." In *The Interpreter's Bible,* edited by G. A. Buttrick et al., 10: 595–749 (New York: Abingdon-Cokesbury Press, 1953).

Bruce, F. F. "The Quintessence of Paulinism." In *Paul: Apostle of the Heart Set Free* (Grand Rapids: Wm. B. Eerdmans Publishing Co., 1977).

Caird, George B. "Ephesians." In *Paul's Letters from Prison.* New Clarendon Bible (Oxford: Oxford University Press, 1976).

Chadwick, Henry. "Die Absicht des Epheserbriefes." *Zeitschrift für die Neutestamentliche Wissenschaft* 51 (1960): 145–153.

Cross, Frank Leslie, ed. *Studies in Ephesians* (London: A. R. Mowbray & Co., 1956).

Goodspeed, Edgar J. *The Meaning of Ephesians* (Chicago: University of Chicago Press, 1933).

Houlden, J. L. "Ephesians." In *Paul's Letters from Prison.* Westminster Pelican Commentaries (Philadelphia: Westminster Press, 1970).

Johnston, George. *Ephesians, Philippians, Colossians and Philemon.* Century Bible (London: Thomas Nelson & Sons, 1967).

Lincoln, Andrew T. *Ephesians.* Word Biblical Commentary (Waco, Tex.: Word Books, 1990).

Mitton, C. Leslie. *The Epistle to the Ephesians: Its Authorship, Origin and Purpose* (Oxford: Clarendon Press, 1951).

———. *Ephesians.* New Century Bible Commentary (Grand Rapids: Wm. B. Eerdmans Publishing Co., 1973).

Patzia, Arthur G. *Colossians, Philemon, Ephesians.* Good News Commentary (San Francisco: Harper & Row, 1984).

Robinson, J. Armitage. *St. Paul's Epistle to the Ephesians.* (London: James Clarke & Co.; New York: Macmillan Co., 1904).

Scott, E. F. *The Epistles of Paul to the Colossians, to Philemon and to the Ephesians.* Moffatt New Testament Commentary (London: Hodder & Stoughton, 1930).

Thompson, G. H. P. *The Letters of Paul to the Ephesians, to the Colossians, and to Philemon.* Cambridge Bible Commentary (Cambridge: Cambridge University Press, 1967).

2. Literature Cited

Arnold, Clinton E. *Ephesians: Power and Magic.* Society for New Testament Studies Monograph Series 63 (Cambridge: Cambridge University Press, 1989).

Baillie, John. *The Belief in Progress* (London: Oxford University Press, 1950).

Barth, Markus. *The Broken Wall: A Study of the Epistle to the Ephesians* (Philadelphia: Judson Press, 1959).

Batey, Richard. "Critical Note: The Destination of Ephesians." *Journal of Biblical Literature* 82 (1963): 101.

Best, Ernest. *One Body in Christ* (London: SPCK, 1955).

――――. "Ephesians i:1." In *Text and Interpretation: Studies in the New Testament presented to Matthew Black,* edited by Ernest Best and R. McL. Wilson (Cambridge: Cambridge University Press, 1979).

Bruce, F. F. *The Epistles to the Colossians, to Philemon, and to the Ephesians.* New International Commentary on the New Testament (Grand Rapids: Wm. B. Eerdmans Publishing Co., 1984).

Bultmann, Rudolf. *"kauchaomai."* In *Theological Dictionary of the New Testament,* edited by Gerhard Kittel; translated by Geoffrey W. Bromiley, 3:645–654 (Grand Rapids: Wm. B. Eerdmans Publishing Co., 1965). Cited as *TDNT.*

――――. *Theology of the New Testament,* vol. 1, translated by Kendrick Grobel (New York: Charles Scribner's Sons, 1951).

Caird, George B. "The Descent of Christ in Ephesians 4:7–11." *Studia Evangelica* II (1964): 535–545.

Dahl, Nils Alstrup. "Early Christian Preaching." In *Jesus in the Memory of the Early Church: Essays by Nils Alstrup Dahl* (Minneapolis: Augsburg Publishing House, 1976).

Dibelius, Martin. *An die Kolosser, Epheser, an Philemon.* Handbuch zum Neuen Testament 12. 3rd ed., rev. by Heinrich Greeven (Tübingen: J. C. B. Mohr [Paul Siebeck], 1953).

Gerstenberger, Erhard S., and Wolfgang Schrage. *Woman and Man.* Biblical Encounter Series (Nashville: Abingdon Press, 1982).

Hanson, Stig. *The Unity of the Church in the New Testament: Colossians and Ephesians* (Stockholm: Almqvist & Wiksells Boktryckeri, 1946).

Hunter, A. M. *Paul and His Predecessors.* New rev. ed. (Philadelphia: Westminster Press, 1961).

Kirby, J. C. *Ephesians, Baptism and Pentecost: An Inquiry Into the Structure and Purpose of the Epistle to the Ephesians* (London: SPCK, 1968).

Lincoln, Andrew T. "The Church and Israel in Ephesians 2." *Catholic Biblical Quarterly* 49 (1987): 605–624.

Martin, Ralph P. "An Epistle in Search of a Life Setting." *Expository Times* 79 (1968): 296–302.

––––––. *New Testament Foundations: A Guide for Christian Students,* vol. 2, rev. ed. (Grand Rapids: Wm. B. Eerdmans Publishing Co., 1978).

Masson, Charles. *L'Epître de Saint Paul aux Ephésiens.* Commentaire du Nouveau Testament 9 (Neuchâtel and Paris: Delachaux & Niestlé, 1953).

Moule, C. F. D. *The Origin of Christology* (Cambridge: Cambridge University Press, 1977).

Murray, Gilbert. "The Failure of Nerve." In *Five Stages of Greek Religion.* 3rd ed. Anchor Books (Garden City, N.Y.: Doubleday & Co., 1955).

Robinson, J. A. T. *The Body: A Study in Pauline Theology.* Studies in Biblical Theology (London: SCM Press, 1952).

Schlier, Heinrich. *Der Brief an die Epheser: Ein Kommentar* (Düsseldorf: Patmos-Verlag, 1957).

Scott, C. A. Anderson. *Christianity According to St. Paul* (Cambridge: Cambridge University Press, 1927).

Zimmerli, Walther. "Concerning the Structure of Old Testament Wisdom." In *Studies in Ancient Israelite Wisdom,* edited by J. L. Cranshaw; translated by B. W. Kovacs (New York: KTAV Publishing House, 1976).

Zuntz, Günter. *The Text of the Epistles: A Disquisition Upon the Corpus Paulinum.* Schweich Lectures of the British Academy, 1946 (London: Oxford University Press, 1953).

Colossians

1. For Further Study

Abbott, T. K. *The Epistles to the Ephesians and to the Colossians.* International Critical Commentary (Edinburgh: T. & T. Clark, 1897).

Caird, George B. "Colossians." In *Paul's Letters from Prison.* New Clarendon Bible (Oxford: Oxford University Press, 1976).

Francis, Fred O., and Wayne A. Meeks, eds. *Conflict at Colossae.* Sources for Biblical Study (Missoula, Mont.: Scholars Press, 1975).

Houlden, J. L. "Colossians." In *Paul's Letters from Prison.* Westminster Pelican Commentaries (Philadelphia: Westminster Press, 1970).

Johnston, George. *Ephesians, Philippians, Colossians and Philemon.* Century Bible (London: Thomas Nelson & Sons, 1967).

Martin, Ralph P. "An Early Christian Hymn (Col. 1:15–20)." *Evangelical Quarterly* 36 (1964): 195–205.

————. "Reconciliation and Forgiveness in the Letter to the Colossians." In *Reconciliation and Hope,* edited by R. Banks (Grand Rapids: Wm. B. Eerdmans Publishing Co., 1974).

Patzia, Arthur G. *Colossians, Philemon, Ephesians.* Good News Commentary (San Francisco: Harper & Row, 1984).

Scott, E. F. *The Epistles of Paul to the Colossians, to Philemon and to the Ephesians.* Moffatt New Testament Commentary (London: Hodder & Stoughton, 1930).

Thompson, G. H. P. *The Letters of Paul to the Ephesians, to the Colossians, and to Philemon.* Cambridge Bible Commentary (Cambridge: Cambridge University Press, 1967).

2. Literature Cited

Berkhof, Hendrik. *Christ and the Powers.* Translated by John H. Yoder (Scottdale, Pa.: Herald Press, 1977).

150   Best, Ernest. *One Body in Christ* (London: SPCK, 1955).

Bieder, Werner. *Die kolossische Irrlehre und die Kirche von heute.* Theologische Studien (Zurich: Evangelischer Verlag, 1952).

Bornkamm, Günther. "The Heresy of Colossians." In *Conflict at Colossae,* edited by Fred O. Francis and Wayne A. Meeks (Missoula, Mont.: Scholars Press, 1975).

Bowen, C. R. "The Original Form of Paul's Letter to the Colossians." *Journal of Biblical Literature* 43 (1924): 177–206.

Bruce, F. F. *Paul: Apostle of the Heart Set Free* (Grand Rapids: Wm. B. Eerdmans Publishing Co., 1977).

————. *The Epistles to the Colossians, to Philemon, and to the Ephesians.* New International Commentary on the New Testament (Grand Rapids: Wm. B. Eerdmans Publishing Co., 1984).

Bujard, W. *Stilanalytische Untersuchungen zum Kolosserbrief als Beitrag zur Methodik von Sprachvergleichen.* Studien zur Umwelt des Neuen Testaments (Göttingen: Vandenhoeck & Ruprecht, 1973).

Cannon, George E. *The Use of Traditional Materials in Colossians* (Macon, Ga.: Mercer University Press, 1983).

Chadwick, H. " 'All Things to All Men.' " *New Testament Studies* 1 (1954–1955): 270–275.

Coutts, J. "The Relationship Between Ephesians and Colossians." *New Testament Studies* 4 (1957–1958): 201–207.

Crouch, James E. *The Origin and Intention of the Colossian Haustafel.* Forschungen zur Religion und Literatur des Alten und Neuen Testaments (Göttingen: Vandenhoeck & Ruprecht, 1972).

Dibelius, Martin. *An die Kolosser, Epheser, an Philemon.* Handbuch zum Neuen Testament 12. 3rd ed., rev. by Heinrich Greeven (Tübingen: J. C. B. Mohr [Paul Siebeck], 1953).

Elliott, John H. "A Catholic Gospel: Reflections on 'Early Catholicism' in the New Testament." *Catholic Biblical Quarterly* 31 (1969): 213–223.

Francis, Fred O. "Visionary Discipline and Scriptural Tradition at Colossae." *Lexington Theological Quarterly* 2 (1967): 71–81.

Fuller, Reginald H. *A Critical Introduction to the New Testament.* Studies in Theology (London: Gerald Duckworth & Co., 1966).

Greeven, Heinrich. *"zēteō."* In *Theological Dictionary of the New Testament,* edited by Gerhard Kittel; translated by

Geoffrey W. Bromiley, 2:892–896 (Grand Rapids: Wm. B. Eerdmans Publishing Co., 1965). Cited as *TDNT.*

Harrison, P. N. "Onesimus and Philemon." *Anglican Theological Review* 32 (1950): 268–294.

Hengel, Martin. "Hymn and Christology." In *Studia Biblica 1978 III: Papers on Paul and Other New Testament Authors,* edited by E. A. Livingstone (Sheffield: Department of Biblical Studies, University of Sheffield, 1980).

Käsemann, Ernst. "A Primitive Christian Baptismal Liturgy." In *Essays in New Testament Themes,* translated by W. S. Montague. Studies in Biblical Theology (Naperville: Alec R. Allenson, 1964).

Kehl, N. *Der Christushymnus im Kolosserbrief: Eine motivgeschichtliche Untersuchung zu Kol 1, 12–20.* Stuttgarter Biblische Monographien (Stuttgart: Katholisches Bibelwerk, 1967).

Kiley, Mark. *Colossians as Pseudepigraphy.* The Biblical Seminar (Sheffield: Journal for the Study of the Old Testament Press, 1986). (See review by Clinton E. Arnold in *Evangelical Quarterly* 60 [1988]: 69–71.)

Klijn, A. F. J. *An Introduction to the New Testament,* translated by M. van der Vathorst-Smit (Leiden: E. J. Brill, 1967).

Knox, John. *Philemon Among the Letters of Paul.* 2d ed. (New York and Nashville: Abingdon Press, 1959).

Lähnemann, Johannes. *Der Kolosserbrief: Komposition, Situation und Argumentation.* Studien zum Neuen Testament (Gütersloh: Gütersloher Verlagshaus Gerd Mohn, 1971).

Lightfoot, J. B. *St. Paul's Epistles to the Colossians and to Philemon* (London: Macmillan, 1879).

Lillie, W. "The Pauline House-tables." *Expository Times* 86 (1974–1975): 179–183.

Lincoln, Andrew T. *Ephesians.* Word Biblical Commentary (Waco, Tex.: Word Books, 1990).

Lohmeyer, E. *Die Briefe an die Philipper, Kolosser und an Philemon.* H. A. W. Meyer, Kritischexegetischer Kommentar über das Neue Testament, 13th ed. (Göttingen: Vandenhoeck & Ruprecht, 1964).

Lohse, Eduard. *Colossians and Philemon,* translated by W. R. Poehlmann and R. J. Karris. Hermeneia (Philadelphia: Fortress Press, 1971).

Malherbe, Abraham J. *Moral Exhortation, A Greco-Roman*

Sourcebook. Library of Early Christianity (Philadelphia: Westminster Press, 1986).

Martin, Ralph P. "Haustafeln." In *New International Dictionary of New Testament Theology,* edited by Colin Brown, 3:928–932 (Grand Rapids: Zondervan Publishing House, 1978, 1986). Cited as *NIDNTT.*

———. "New Testament Hymns." *Expository Times* 94 (1983): 132–136.

———. *Reconciliation: A Study of Paul's Theology.* Rev. ed. (Grand Rapids: Academie Books, Zondervan Publishing House, 1989).

Marxsen, Willi. *Introduction to the New Testament: An Approach to Its Problems,* translated by G. Buswell (Philadelphia: Fortress Press, 1968).

Masson, Charles. *L'Epître de Saint Paul aux Colossiens.* Commentaire du Nouveau Testament (Neuchâtel and Paris: Delachaux & Niestlé, 1953).

Mayerhoff, Ernst T. *Der Brief an die Colosser, mit vornehmlicher Berücksichtigung der drei Pastoralbriefe kritisch geprüft* (Berlin: H. Schultze, 1838).

Moule, C. F. D. *The Epistles of Paul the Apostle to the Colossians and to Philemon.* Cambridge Greek Testament Commentary (Cambridge: Cambridge University Press, 1957).

O'Brien, Peter T. *Colossians-Philemon.* Word Biblical Commentary (Waco, Tex.: Word Books, 1982).

Oepke, Albrecht. *"egeirō."* In *Theological Dictionary of the New Testament,* edited by Gerhard Kittel; translated by Geoffrey W. Bromiley, 3:333–339 (Grand Rapids: Wm. B. Eerdmans Publishing Co., 1965).

Percy, E. *Die Probleme der Kolosser- und Epheserbriefe* (Lund: C. W. K. Gleerup, 1946).

Robinson, B. W. "An Ephesian Imprisonment of Paul." *Journal of Biblical Literature* 29 (1910): 181–189.

Schweizer, Eduard. *The Letter to the Colossians: A Commentary,* translated by Andrew Chester (Minneapolis: Augsburg Publishing House, 1982).

Stewart, James S. "A First-Century Heresy and Its Modern Counterpart." *Scottish Journal of Theology* 23 (1970): 420–436.

Synge, F. C. *Philippians and Colossians.* 2nd ed. Torch Bible Commentaries (London: SCM Press, 1958).

Wink, Walter. *Naming the Powers: The Language of Power in the New Testament* (Philadelphia: Fortress Press, 1984).

Wright, N. T. *Colossians and Philemon.* Tyndale New Testament Commentaries (Grand Rapids: Wm. B. Eerdmans Publishing Co., 1986).

Philemon

1. For Further Study

Caird, George B. "Philemon." In *Paul's Letters from Prison.* New Clarendon Bible (Oxford: Oxford University Press, 1976).

Houlden, J. L. "Philemon." In *Paul's Letters from Prison.* Westminster Pelican Commentaries (Philadelphia: Westminster Press, 1970).

Johnston, George. *Ephesians, Philippians, Colossians and Philemon.* Century Bible (London: Thomas Nelson & Sons, 1967).

Lohse, E. *Colossians and Philemon,* translated by W. R. Poehlmann and R. J. Karris. Hermeneia (Philadelphia: Fortress Press, 1971).

Müller, Jac. J. *The Epistles of Paul to the Philippians and to Philemon.* New International Critical Commentary on the New Testament (Grand Rapids: Wm. B. Eerdmans Publishing Co., 1955).

Patzia, Arthur G. *Colossians, Philemon, Ephesians.* Good News Commentary (San Francisco: Harper & Row, 1984).

Scott, E. F. *The Epistles of Paul to the Colossians, to Philemon and to the Ephesians.* Moffatt New Testament Commentary (London: Hodder & Stoughton, 1930).

Thompson, G. H. P. *The Letters of Paul to the Ephesians, to the Colossians, and to Philemon.* Cambridge Bible Commentary (Cambridge: Cambridge University Press, 1967).

Wright, N. T. *Colossians and Philemon.* Tyndale New Testament Commentaries (Grand Rapids: Wm. B. Eerdmans Publishing Co., 1986).

2. Literature Cited

154   Bruce, F. F. "St. Paul in Rome. 2. The Epistle to Philemon." *Bulletin of the John Rylands University Library of Manchester* 48 (1965–1966):81–97.

Derrett, J. Duncan M. "The Functions of the Epistle to Philemon." *Zeitschrift für die neutestamentliche Wissenschaft* 79 (1988): 63–91.

Dibelius, Martin. *An die Kolosser, Epheser, an Philemon.* Handbuch zum Neuen Testament 12. 3rd ed., rev. by Heinrich Greeven (Tübingen: J. C. B. Mohr [Paul Siebeck], 1953).

Dodd, C. H. "The Mind of Paul: Change and Development." *Bulletin of the John Rylands University Library of Manchester* 18 (1934): 69–110. Reprinted in *New Testament Studies* (Manchester: Manchester University Press, 1953), pp. 83–128.

Doty, William G. *Letters in Primitive Christianity.* Guides to Biblical Scholarship (Philadelphia: Fortress Press, 1973).

Duncan, G. S. *St. Paul's Ephesian Ministry* (New York: Charles Scribner's Sons, 1929).

Goodenough, E. R. "Paul and Onesimus." *Harvard Theological Review* 22 (1929): 181–183.

Greeven, Heinrich. "Prüfung des Thesen von J. Knox zum Philemonbrief." *Theologische Literaturzeitung* 79 (1954): 373–378.

Grenfell, B. P., and A. S. Hunt, eds. *The Oxyrhynchus Papyri,* vol. 14 (London: Egypt Exploration Society, 1920).

Haenchen, Ernst. *The Acts of the Apostles, A Commentary,* translated by Bernard Noble, Gerald Shinn, et al. (Philadelphia: Westminster Press, 1971).

Harrison, P. N. "Onesimus and Philemon." *Anglican Theological Review* 32 (1950): 268–294.

Knox, John. *Philemon Among the Letters of Paul.* 2d ed. (New York and Nashville: Abingdon Press, 1959).

Lehrmann, R. *Epître à Philémon* (Geneva: Labor et Fides, 1978).

Lightfoot, J. B. *St. Paul's Epistles to the Colossians and to Philemon* (London: Macmillan, 1879).

Moule, C. F. D. *The Epistles of Paul the Apostle to the Colossians and to Philemon.* Cambridge Greek Testament Commentary (Cambridge: Cambridge University Press, 1957).

Petersen, Norman R. *Rediscovering Paul: Philemon and the Sociology of Paul's Narrative World* (Philadelphia: Fortress Press, 1985).

Preiss, Théo. "Life in Christ and Social Ethics in the Epistle to Philemon." In *Life in Christ,* translated by Harold Knight.

155

Studies in Biblical Theology (Chicago: Alec R. Allenson, 1954).

Scott, C. A. Anderson. *Saint Paul the Man and the Teacher.* Rev. ed. (Cambridge: Cambridge University Press, 1936).

Winter, Sara C. "Paul's Letter to Philemon." *New Testament Studies* 33 (1987): 1–15.